D1307830

MILLENNIALS VS. BOOMERS

Listen, Learn, and SUCCEED Together

**Eric Harvey &
Silvana Clark**

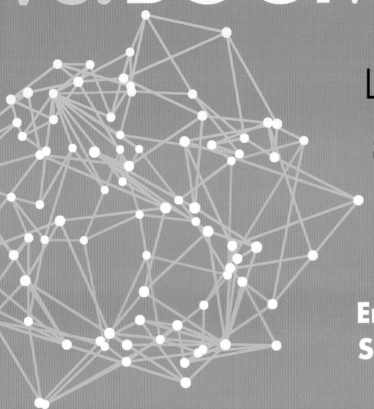

simple ▶ truths®

small books. BIG IMPACT.

Photo Credits
Cover: AntartStock/Shutterstock
Internals: page 1 AntartStock/Shutterstock; pages 8–9, phipatbig/Shutterstock, Creative-idea/iStock; pages 10–11, teerayut tae/Shutterstock; pages 37, 45, 53, 61, 69, 77, 83, 99, 107, Ingka D. Jiw/Shutterstock.

Published by Simple Truths, an imprint of Sourcebooks, Inc.
P.O. Box 4410, Naperville, Illinois 60567-4410
(630) 961-3900
Fax: (630) 961-2168
www.sourcebooks.com

Printed and bound in China.

QL 10 9 8 7 6 5 4 3 2

Millennials now represent the largest generation in the United States, comprising almost one-quarter of the total population... and growing!

MILLENNIALS
VS.
BOOMERS

Listen, Learn, and Succeed Together

n today's workplace we often have a coworker population that can represent age gaps of forty-plus years. With that range comes a host of different experiences, expectations, and perspectives. *Millennials vs. Boomers* will give readers a better understanding and appreciation of viewpoint differences in these important workplace areas:

MILLENNIALS VS BOOMERS

This powerful resource represents workplace viewpoints from two perspectives. One side will cover the experiences and attitudes of your newer employees, aka Millennials, while the other side of the book covers the perspectives of your "seasoned" employees, aka Baby Boomers.

Millennials vs. Boomers is designed to bridge perception differences and viewpoint gaps. This book will help you create more understanding and acceptance of ideas, while ensuring more success for individuals, work teams, and the entire organization.

Dear Boomer,

We are the younger employee and colleague you deal with. We are affectionately known as Millennials, and we represent a significant population of people you work with every day. Some of us are your coworkers, some of us direct reports, and a few of us are even your managers.

We may have different sizes, shapes, colors, beliefs, and experiences. We are younger and more technology focused than you and your contemporaries. Our age differences can and do cause different viewpoints to naturally occur. Neither of us is typically absolutely right and the other absolutely wrong, but certainly our viewpoints may be quite different. Those differences can become strengths or become weakness depending on how they are appreciated and how they are managed.

Just like you and your fellow Boomers, I want to be understood, accepted, and appreciated for how I have performed to date and especially how much more I can contribute in the future. For that to occur we both need to do a better job of understanding and appreciating our different viewpoints.

The following pages are about opening up to you—about sharing my feelings on many aspects of my job and working with you. This new information, I hope, will encourage you to see me in a new, and perhaps different, light.

Please listen to these messages with the same level of compassion and understanding that you wish from me as I read the flip side of this book. Chances are we will both discover new insights about our different viewpoints and work together more effectively.

We have different

personalities and different

skills and the kind of

things that we do, we can do together that neither of us can do separately.

Guy Burgess

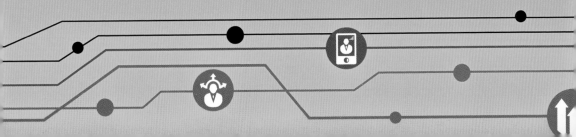

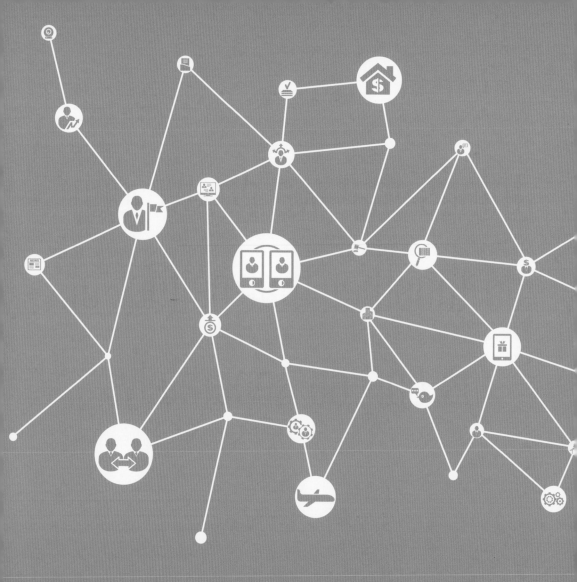

TEAMWORK AND WORKING TOGETHER

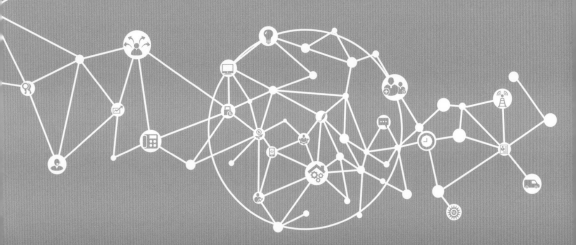

Teamwork is the ability to work together toward a common vision. The ability to direct individual accomplishments toward organizational objectives. It is the fuel that allows common people to attain uncommon results.

Andrew Carnegie

There's a popular motivational poster that says "There's no 'I' in TEAM." We agree! Ever since we were little, we've worked in groups ranging from sports activities to chess clubs to dance classes. Even in high school a bunch of us would go to the movies as a group, instead of pairing off as couples. (Don't worry. Most of us eventually found that someone special!) Instead of individual term papers, teachers often assigned us group projects, which kept us happily engaged.

I have lots of ideas, but I like someone to bounce these ideas off of. I don't like being rejected, and I frequently seek others' buy-in and input before I make decisions. Once we narrow down an idea, project, or program, I am happy to work by myself to make it happen. However, I prefer people around me to provide feedback and affirmation that I am moving in the right direction. When you are part of the team, I get a different perspective than I do when I'm with people my own age. I must say you do come up with good ideas too!

On the job, working as a team makes sense. We hear feedback on our ideas right away. It's fun to get everyone's opinions even if some ideas are totally off the wall. There's a certain camaraderie when we work together on a project, bantering and laughing. Often that camaraderie spills over to after-work hours. It isn't unusual for someone to get a text from a team member late at night, suggesting a new twist on a work project that had us all stumped. Teams are created for collaboration. Instead of being given a directive and having to carry out the task by myself, I can get input from my team members. This creates an environment where everyone has the freedom to collaborate and contribute to the project.

You might think we're just goofing around if three or four of us are talking together. Sure, we might be briefly discussing the great new food truck that just arrived on the next block, but more than likely we're actually talking about a work-related issue. Teamwork means many things. It's possible we're working together on a project that includes people in our organization with years of experience as well as that just-arrived new employee. Other times teamwork means two of us complete the assignment while twelve coworkers are busily completing another task.

No matter the size or skill level of each team, they are all built on trust. The more we work together, the more positive, trusting relationships we develop. This in turn creates team members willing to take creative risks because we know the team backs us up. Will everyone agree with our ideas? Probably not. Yet a strong team creates that "safe place" for us all to feel our opinions are valued. Not always accepted, but valued! Being part of a team also softens the blow when we aren't as successful as we thought we'd be!

Teamwork involves working toward a common goal. With individual people focused on reaching that goal together, we become a successful team. All of us want to be heard and respected for our work. Growing up, we learned the importance of acknowledging each other's strengths. Working as a team helps us share ideas and look for creative solutions to problems.

Teamwork builds trust, talent, and enables us to accomplish important tasks.

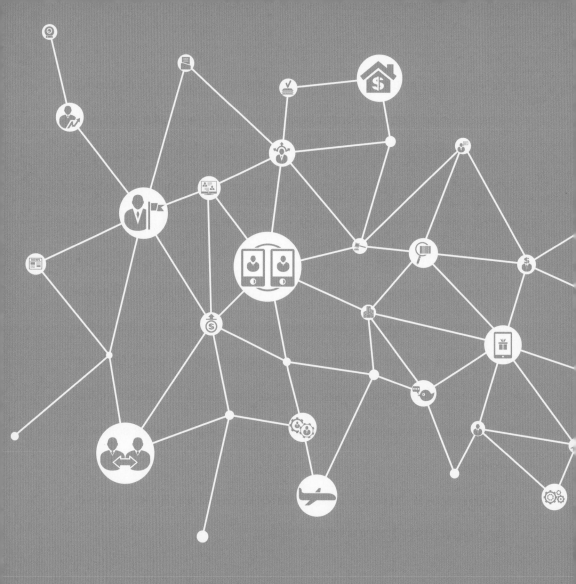

LOYALTY TO THE JOB AND THE ORGANIZATION

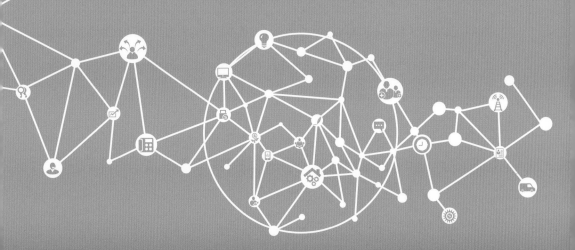

> *The thing I was attracted to as a little girl was Kirk, Bones, and Spock, and their utter loyalty. There's nothing more powerful than that.*

Jolene Blalock

My dad worked for the same organization for twenty-five years. Sometimes he'd come home and complain about a new major policy change or tell us stories about the boss from hell. We'd simply ask him, "Why don't you just quit?" This resulted in an extended lecture about the importance of job loyalty. He felt obligated to stay at the organization because it offered him a decent salary and benefits so he could provide for his family. Looking back, I never appreciated the sacrifice he made for us by staying with an unfulfilling job.

If company loyalty means having to stay at a job that I don't enjoy, then company loyalty is not for me. Oh, I know everyone has off days when they think their jobs suck. But for me, if my job turns into a daily grind of frustration and stress, I want out. Why should I face each day with dread of going to work? To me, a job is a source of personal fulfillment and a paycheck. I want to work for a socially responsible organization that values my skills. Because of my age though, I have time and the flexibility to be selective about the jobs I take. I'll never be a time-card puncher like my dad.

To me, loyalty is a two-way street. When I see management working hard to create a positive, forward-moving organization, then I'm in! If I get the feeling I was hired just to do grunt work, with little chance for advancement, I certainly don't plan on sticking around very long. It's important to me that I have a chance to further my career and be with an organization that tries to hire from within. That gives me the desire to be loyal and stay with my job because of the possibility of a promotion.

(And a raise!) My loyalty increases as I'm given more responsibility and opportunities for additional training.

Want to know what else would help me become a loyal employee? Show me how my job impacts others or the world. Obviously we can't all work at organizations that feed inner-city children or build wells in remote African villages. But if I learn about some ways our organization supports and gives back to the community, my loyalty increases. I want to work for an organization that cares about more than just making a profit. Let me know about our core values and future goals. Keep me informed on ways my job makes an impact, however small, on the lives of others.

Sometimes I hear rumors on the job about cutting back on hours or even layoffs. How can I be loyal when I'm trying to figure out if I'll be let go next week? Open communication gives me the confidence to know the organization is prompt to dispel rumors by being forthright with all of us. Believe me, all it takes is one little rumor to get me busy on the computer searching for another job! My loyalty disappears at the possibility of unemployment.

Relationships in my personal and professional life play a part in determining my loyalty. If I'm working with people who genuinely care about my success at work, I'm more likely to stay with the organization. By having role models who inspire me to do my best at work, I develop a desire to grow with the organization. I enjoy the feeling of connected-ness I get when working as a team; no one wants to work in a vacuum. Loyalty increases as all of us create a positive working environment. A relationship with coworkers based on trust and open communication is one reason I'm more likely to stay with the organization.

The more people understand what's going on and how they contribute, the more loyal they become.

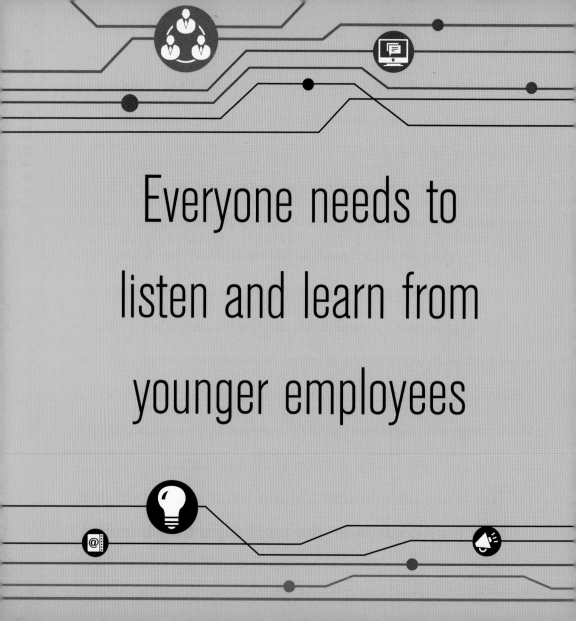

because their ideas often lead to important innovations and faster growth opportunities.

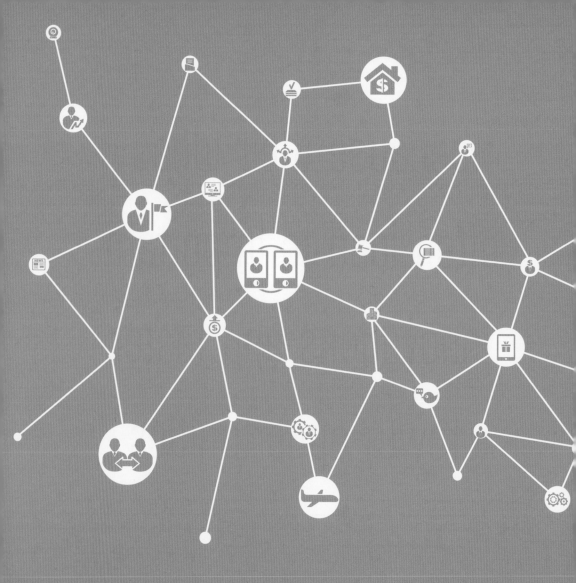

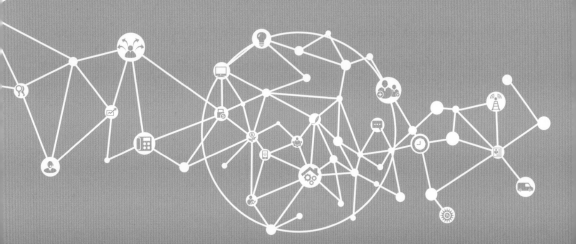

DEALING WITH CHANGE

The world is constantly changing, so it makes sense to change as individuals. Our parents constantly tell us how quickly life changed after the "invention" of the Internet. Instead of learning cursive to write a report in elementary school, we hunted and pecked away on a school computer and printed the report on an inkjet printer. Now we see change on a daily basis as we find new ways to communicate with photos, blogs, tweets, and iWatches. We've always known a world where life seems to happen faster and faster. I can take a picture of myself and have my friends around the world see me in seconds. It's also possible to instantly access a YouTube video on how to tie a tie.

Most people hear the word "change" and get worried. But change can be positive. How about when you get a raise or meet the love of your life? Those are great changes. At work, we often hear people say, "We don't need to change. We've always done it this way." True. The status quo might work for some things. (It's probably always a good idea to keep your hand off a hot stove.) Yet making some changes might even increase work productivity. Think how efficient it is to have computerized files for staff names or supply lists. Back in the Dark Ages, you probably hand-wrote all those documents.

Many organizations seem resistant to change. After all, they had to be doing something right to grow and expand. In fact, I'm sometimes amazed at how some organizations have been able to have employees and make a profit while using so many outdated methods. They have my respect for getting this far with basic supplies and equipment. However, that situation cannot last forever.

I get the sense you are sometimes hesitant to change work habits. You get frustrated when we don't see things the same way you do. We Millennials have grown up in a world where change happens so fast that it seems natural to us. We expect to change our smartphones on a regular basis. We expect to change careers many times in our lives. It's difficult for us to understand why change at work has to be so process-oriented and move at lethargic speed. Often we hear Boomers say, "We really should change the way we do this." But then everything stays the same. Change requires action, even if that action is stressful or time-consuming at first.

Today many organizations run by younger employers are growing at a rapid pace. We need to see these trends and capitalize on them. This flexibility to change keeps us invigorated and excited to see where the future takes us. We don't want to work for a stagnant organization! People who embrace change should be valued and seen as flexible, adaptable team players.

You can see how we get frustrated on the job when we have a great idea but run into roadblocks when trying to implement it. All we hear people say is, "That will never work," "We've always done it *this* way," or "We tried that before and it didn't work." Is change really that hard? You and your Boomer buddies gave us a great base to have a successful organization. Could we start with making some minor changes? Those small changes can work on top of your experienced base and develop into major changes, making us an even more successful organization.

CHANGE IS POSITIVE! So please listen to some of our ideas, and we can work together to create some outstanding outcomes together.

Effective communication is

the ability to build

USA:

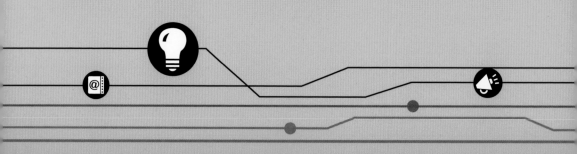

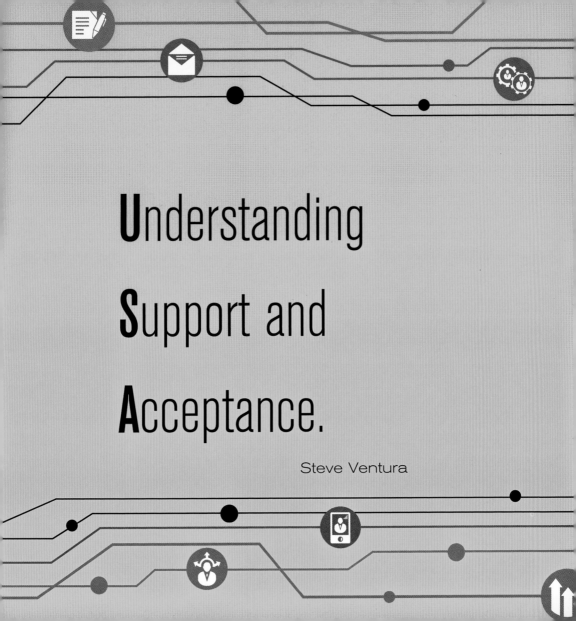

Understanding

Support and

Acceptance.

Steve Ventura

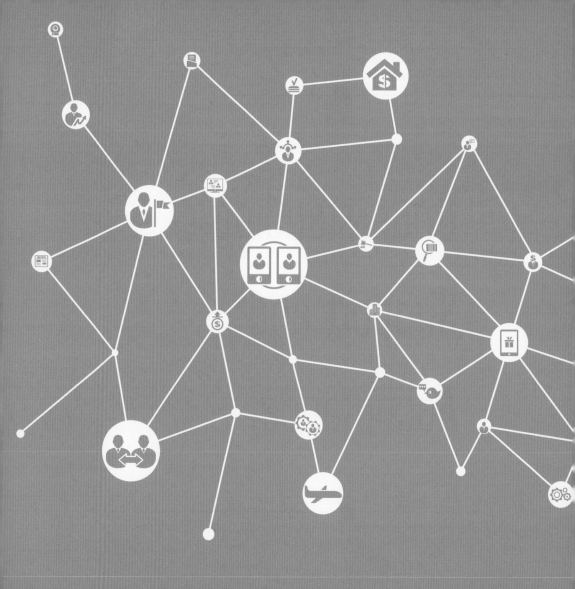

THE QUALITY AND QUANTITY OF COMMUNICATION

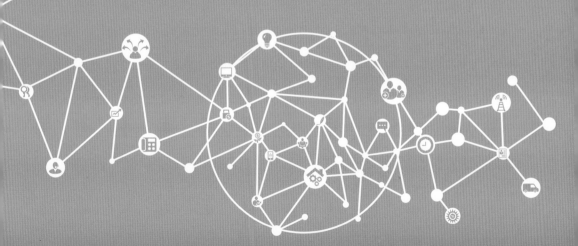

f a friend gets a promotion I know about it instantly through social media. Within minutes I can coordinate a tailgate party with a few taps on my smartphone. Communication for me is quick. That's why it's hard for me to understand why I am sometimes left in the dark about what is happening at work. When I don't get all the information about a project, or hear rumors about forthcoming changes, I feel like a cog in a machine rather than a valued part of your team.

Also, I want to be told I'm doing a great job, and I can take some constructive criticism as well. I don't expect to be told every day how great I am, but I do want *some* feedback. Compared to you, I'm fairly new to the work environment, and I can't always tell whether I'm meeting expectations or performing adequately. Annual or quarterly reviews are helpful, but I need feedback on a more consistent basis to feel confident in my job.

I am pretty good at effectively multitasking. Doing several things at the same time is just the way I operate! Even when walking past someone in the hall, I can have a short conversation with someone and feel I've communicated effectively. Yes, there are times you need to give me information—but make it fast and let me get back to my job. Sometimes when we have long staff meetings, I have the feeling we waste a lot of time presenting information that could have been more effectively summed up in an email or a text. My generation communicates in a different way. Even in high school, we'd get an email from a teacher with pertinent information. We didn't need to be in class to communicate with her.

At work, I sometimes hear you say, "My door is open. Come talk to me anytime." Yet the few times I've gone to talk over an idea with you, I get the feeling you are just placating me and waiting until I leave so you can get back to "important" business. Sometimes nonverbal communication, such as looking at your watch or glancing at paperwork, conveys you aren't really interested in what I'm saying. I'd like to be able to trust you and believe what you say. Help me understand the best time and place to communicate with you. Communication is more than simply exchanging information…it's understanding the emotion (and sometimes the frustration) behind the words. We say one thing and the other person hears another thing. That even happens when sending an email, because it's hard to understand the tone in a short written message.

I know you are busy, but I'd appreciate it if you'd occasionally stop by and ask about something in my personal life. (Not too personal though!) Do you know I volunteer to help at-risk teens get their GEDs? Maybe you could send me a short email letting me know about an upcoming project you think I might be interested in. I may have some great input! Effective communication is the key to building a loyal and dedicated workforce. It's more than staff meetings, memos, or face-to-face conversation.

When it comes to communication, we don't always have to agree. The simple act of listening and understanding the emotions behind the words will surely improve understanding.

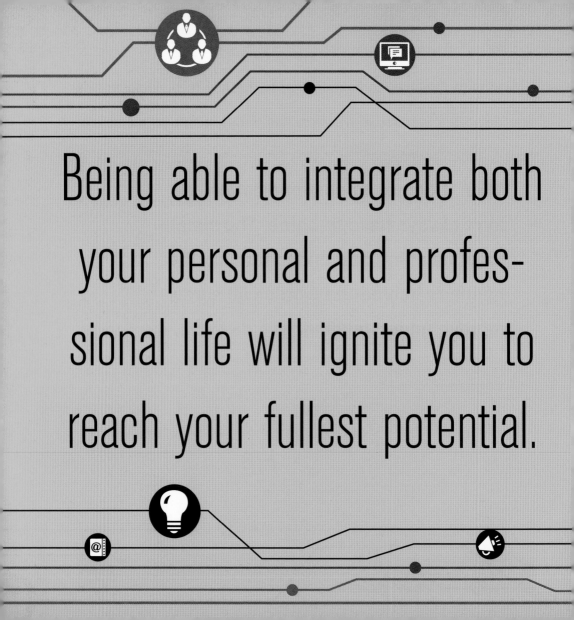

Being able to integrate both your personal and profes-sional life will ignite you to reach your fullest potential.

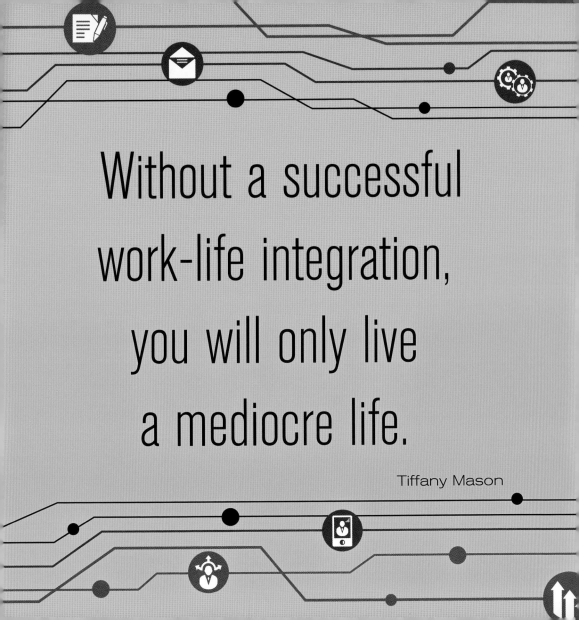

Without a successful work-life integration, you will only live a mediocre life.

Tiffany Mason

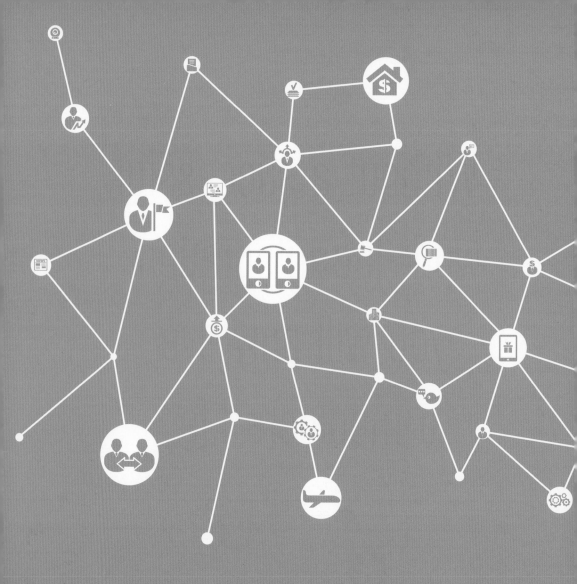

WORK-LIFE BALANCE

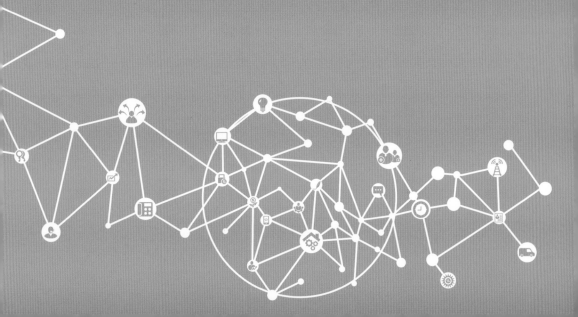

My friends and I believe in the motto "Work hard, play hard." We don't mind coming in early to help out with a special project if it means we will get the job done well. We want to prove our worth and be seen as valuable members of the team. But when that means routinely working longer hours and constantly getting increased responsibilities outside our normal job responsibly, our work-life balance is thrown way out of whack.

Boomers often have the belief that Millennials can work longer hours because we don't have as many family obligations. While it is true that our off-the-job time may be used differently, we still have many social, professional, and community activities that are important to us. Happier, balanced employees are also more productive and tend to stay with an organization longer.

Work-life balance doesn't mean we are counting our exact overtime minutes and want an equal amount of time off. If we work extra hours for a few weeks during a busy time, then it's nice to know we're entitled to some considerations when business slows down. Most organizations have times when everyone needs to put in extra time and effort. How about we bring in some pizzas when we are too busy to go out for lunch? Speaking of lunch, I often see you at noon, munching on a bag of vending machine chips while sitting at your desk. When I take a lunch break to visit with a friend at a nearby coffee shop, I come back to work refreshed. However, I then feel torn because I believe you may not feel it's appropriate to take time for a "real" lunch break.

When my work-life balance is off-kilter, my stress increases. Naturally that affects my work performance, because who can work effectively when they feel ready to snap? My dad used to have a very clear distinction between work and home. Once he left his organization, he was done for the day. No checking emails or texting coworkers about some minor work-related issues! (Sure, email and text messages didn't exist back then, but you get my point.) He left work *at* work. When he got home, he relaxed in his recliner for a while and then came outside to toss the football with us.

It wouldn't make sense to have a clear, distinct fifty-fifty split of equal time at work and home. That's where the balance comes into play. By allowing for scheduled downtime, I'm able to recharge and get energized to be a more productive team member at work. I believe we could all benefit from this.

There isn't a one-size-fits-all approach to achieving work-life balance. Those of us without family responsibilities may find it easier to occasionally put in overtime hours. However, I see you putting in longer and longer hours while complaining you never have time for your family. How does that make sense? Work-life balance can be in a state of flux. Sometimes organizations have peak times where employees need to give extra time and effort. When that peak period levels out, it's time to plug in some "me" time. Make an effort to balance the complexities of work with time for family, hobbies, and an occasional vacation. You'll come back ready to give 100 percent at work. Plus we'll enjoy being around you when you're not so stressed out!

Let's work together to find ways to tip the scales toward producing less on-the-job stress and building more work-life balance.

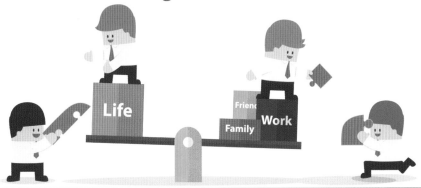

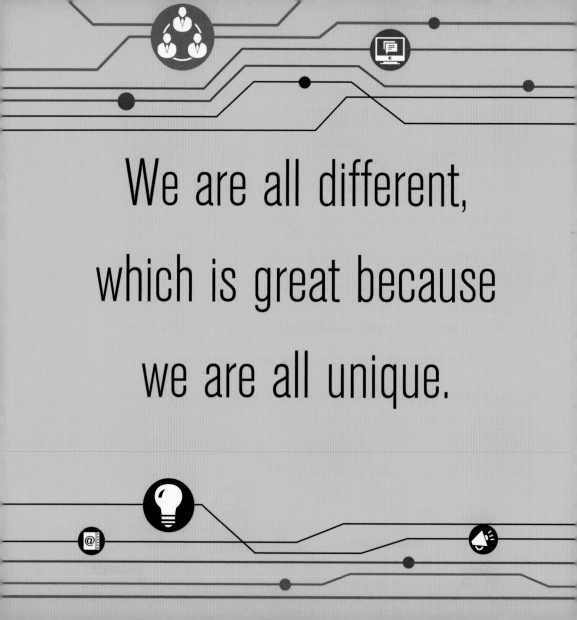

We are all different, which is great because we are all unique.

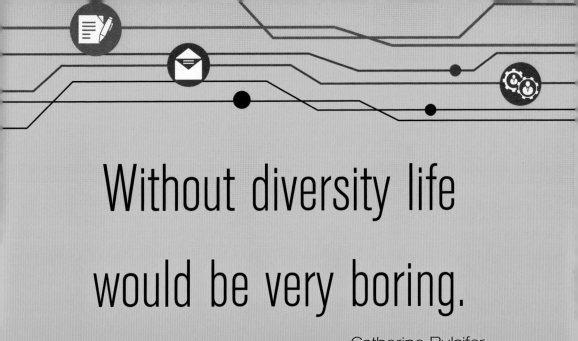

Without diversity life
would be very boring.

Catherine Pulsifer

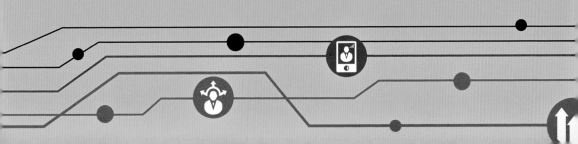

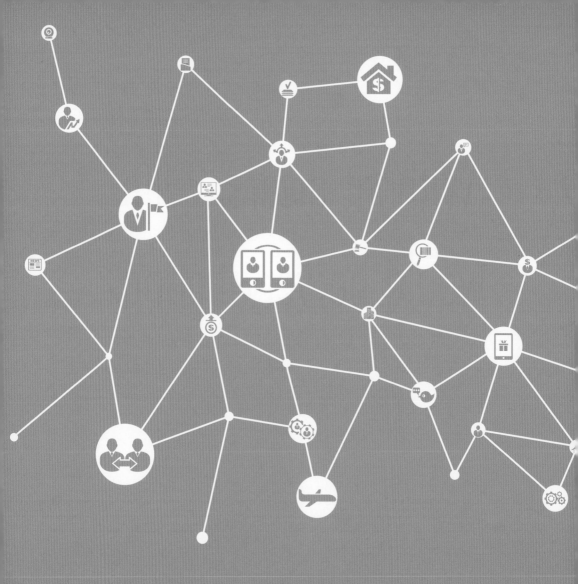

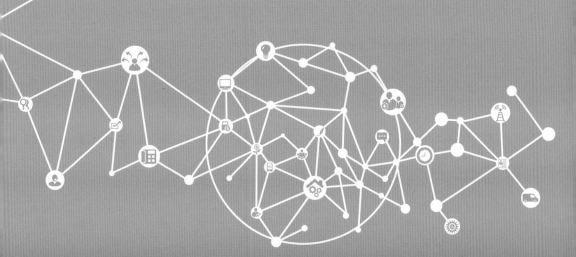

DIVERSITY
AND
INCLUSION

n middle school we put on the play *Annie*. Traditionally this play was about a spunky, redheaded girl living in an orphanage with eight Caucasian orphans. Our production had an African-American Annie with an assortment of Asian, Indian, and Hispanic orphans. Since our school was pretty diverse, it all seemed perfectly normal to me. Then my grandmother came to the play and whispered (rather loudly), "Why aren't there any white girls onstage?" Grandma obviously had never sat in on a diversity training! She explained later how the world has changed from her time growing up on a farm in Iowa where everyone looked the same. That helped me understand why some older employees sometimes convey discomfort when working with people who look and act different.

Diversity and inclusion play a key role in business success. By hiring employees with different backgrounds and cultures, we get an amazing pool of talent. Instead of seeing the world from a typical middle-class viewpoint, we find ourselves hearing about lifestyles and experiences that give all of us a broader view of the world. To me, that makes sense. It's easy for me to see the value in having a diverse workforce.

Unfortunately not everyone in our organization feels the same way. Sometimes people from different religious, ethnic, or gender groups make a few of our coworkers uncomfortable. I've seen the looks on some employees' faces if they get assigned to work on a team with a person who looks or dresses a bit out of their norm. There's a wariness and uncertainty to working with someone who not only looks different, but also speaks or acts different. Instead of being a blue-eyed, blond Caucasian wearing khakis and a button-down dress shirt, these people may wear a sarong and even bring some unique-smelling food for lunch the people in the office have never seen before. I'm not saying all Millennials are accepting people. Some have prejudices; it's true. On the whole though, most of us have grown up being exposed in person or through the media to people of many colors, sizes, sexual orientations, and gender identities.

Just as we learn from people with different years of experience in the workplace, we learn from people with different cultures. Often you hear someone say, "We're all people, so we're all alike." Actually, we're all different. We have different beliefs, different customs, different religious beliefs, different clothing styles, and different dreams for the future. Diversity is the main thing we have in common; so let's accept that. We can all be proud of our differences.

Organizations gain strength by working with our similarities as well as our differences. We create a synergistic work environment by including people with diverse backgrounds. It's easier for me, simply because I've grown up with seeing diversity on TV and social media. I know not everyone lives in a cute house with a white picket fence. By making a strong effort to recruit a diverse workforce, we grow and keep up with the way society is changing. Think how boring it would be if we all looked and thought alike. Let's celebrate our differences! Let's reduce conflict by highlighting the strengths and talents we all have, regardless of personal demographics.

Together Millennials and Boomers can be leaders and collaborators in the areas of diversity and inclusion.

Everyone has an invisible sign hanging

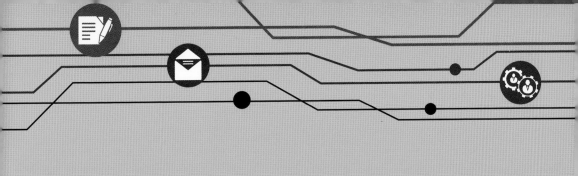

from their neck saying,

"Make Me Feel Important!"

Mary Kay Ash

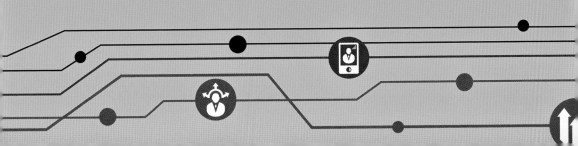

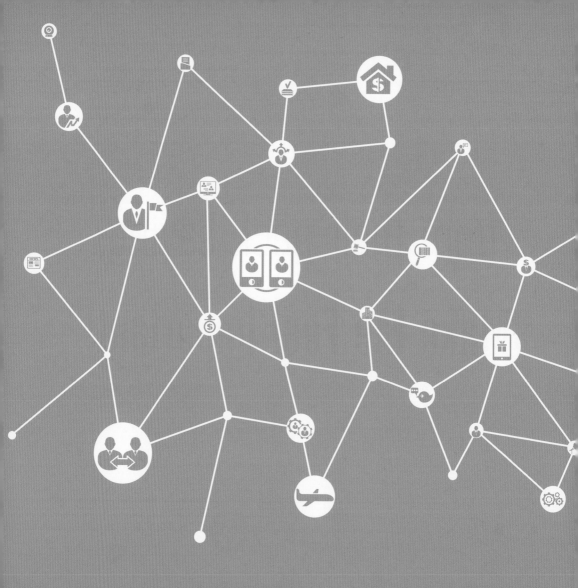

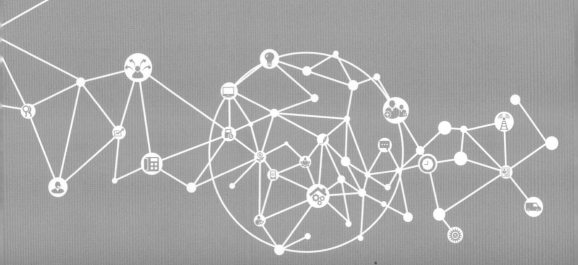

REWARDS AND RECOGNITION

My mom loves to tell how she used flash cards when I was a toddler to help me learn the names of dinosaurs. From there my parents helped coach my sports teams and drove me to countless extracurricular activities. My parents are my friends and mentors. Not only did we have fun together, but they also acknowledged my accomplishments in school, activities, and volunteer work. During high school, my teachers (and even my principal) would give me recognition for things I did. Maybe that's why I'm used to having someone tell me they noticed that I reached a goal or accomplished something noteworthy. People my age grew up getting a trophy just for *participating* on a soccer team and had signs on our lawn saying things like, "Erika is a member of the drum line."

Lots of my friends have interned for free at different companies, working forty or more hours a week. Yes, we are glad to get a "real" job, but we've also put in our time helping our organization. A little recognition isn't too much to ask. By being recognized for our accomplishments, we get motivated to continue being a valued employee. Don't we all like to be noticed for our efforts? Yes, there's value in doing a good job simply because that's what we are paid to do. I do make an effort to reach my goals and often go above and beyond my specific responsibilities. What I'm asking for is an occasional, old-fashioned pat on the back. Or as my dad would say, "Attah Boy!" (Or Girl!)

I understand everyone is busy, but let's try to occasionally give each other positive feedback on how we are doing. For example, you could send me an email that says, "Thanks for coming early to help me set up my presentation yesterday." I do work hard and would just like to be recognized for my contributions and accomplishments. This might be a hard idea to grasp. When you entered the workforce, people probably didn't see the need to offer recognition to coworkers. Now I'm asking you to give me something you didn't necessarily experience yourself.

One of the reasons we frequently change jobs is lack of recognition. It's been proven that organizations that have recognition and a positive reinforcement culture in place have employees who stay longer. They feel more engaged, which obviously results in better serving customers. When you acknowledge us for a job well-done, it lifts our spirits.

Getting recognized for achievement helps put job stress into perspective. Who wants to come to work if all day is spent at a computer or behind a counter, doggedly completing job-related tasks without any recognition? Like Mary Poppins says, "A spoonful of sugar makes the medicine go down." A little "sweetness" from you would make a big impact in my job performance. I'll make an effort to recognize your accomplishments as well!

Some organizations have an employee of the month program. That's a nice touch, but what about providing people with more learning and self-development opportunities? Personal and professional development is a great form of recognition. What about some fun awards such as being recognized for having the most creative screensaver, or writing the funniest post on the company's Facebook page? I'm not asking for a professional comedian to perform at lunch (although we'd all love to see Tina Fey perform in the staff room next week).

By looking for little ways to give recognition to each other, our organization gains big rewards in the form of engaged and creative employees.

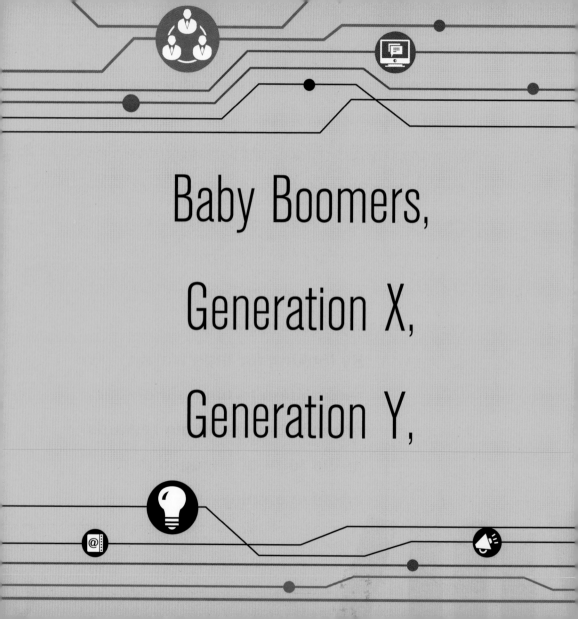

Baby Boomers,

Generation X,

Generation Y,

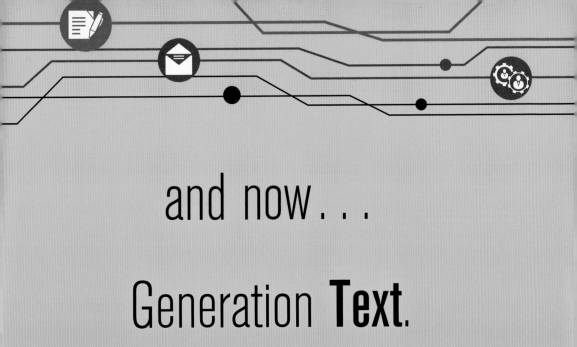

and now. . .

Generation **Text.**

Greg Tamblyn

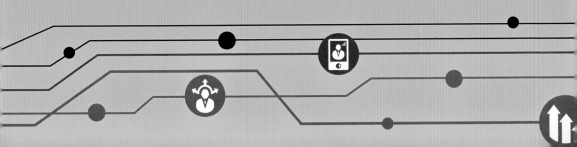

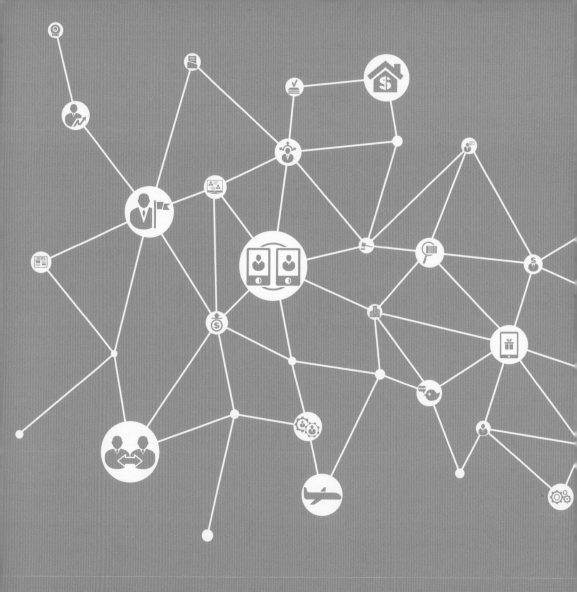

DEALING WITH TECHNOLOGY

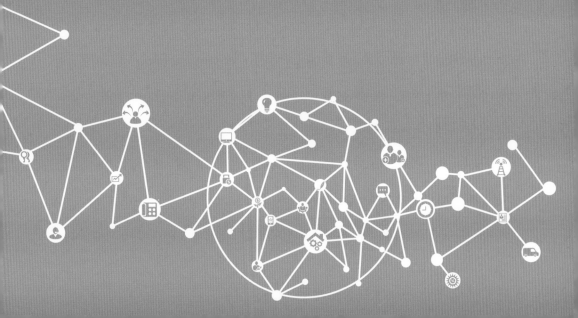

won't lie. Technology comes easy to us. In fourth grade, we had a computer lab. Once a week senior citizens would come to our elementary school and we'd teach them how to use the Internet and email. I remember trying not to laugh when a sweet elderly lady kept picking up the mouse and pointing it at the computer screen, thinking it worked like a remote for the TV. She marveled when I showed her how to download a recipe for apple pie. All through school, most of our education involved using technology in some way. Is it any wonder it seems natural to me to use technology for communicating at work with you? Why not use a quick text to change the time of meeting rather than a phone call or voice message?

Technology is here to stay. It's easy to contact ten of my friends with one text and plan a get-together. I am used to unlimited information at my fingertips. (Or even at my voice command.) I'm also used to multitasking.

At home and at work, it's easy for me to work on my computer, check my email at work, post a picture, and text a friend to come over for dinner that I made with help from a recipe on Pinterest. I like to have something going on all the time. Often I send a quick text while waiting for a website to load.

Change is often scary. I see the effort you make trying to keep up with new apps, software upgrades, social media platforms, and other technology advancements. While all those things come naturally to me, I understand there's a learning curve for you. Sometimes it's a steep curve! Technology has impacted all aspects of our lives. It's also changed the way we do things. Instead of having an alarm clock, my smartphone blasts a cheery tune to get me out of bed. Where you once might have carried a yellow legal pad to meetings, it's now easier to jot notes on your laptop.

Staff members who are less experienced with technology often take jabs at us because of our technological expertise. Yet when one of you needs help setting up a computer program or even just managing a spreadsheet, who do you call? It's simply assumed we will take time away from our job duties to fix any of your computer problems. I don't mind helping out occasionally, but please reciprocate by learning a bit more about technology yourself.

I realize that an overwhelming amount of information can cause confusion. I see many of you getting stressed with new hardware and software. I would be happy to help you with this dilemma; just ask and I'll try to point you in the right direction to get the solutions you need. Next time tech support is at your desk, ask them to explain what they are doing and how you can avoid calling them next time. Did you know there are basic online training courses explaining the mysteries of our technology?

We all have the same goal of working with a successful organization. Technology offers awesome ways to streamline our practices and procedures. So, rather than getting frustrated at the complexities of technology, let's look at working together to benefit from all that technology has to offer us.

Let's make a deal: I will stop texting if you agree to listen to what I have to say about new technology opportunities for our organization.

• • •

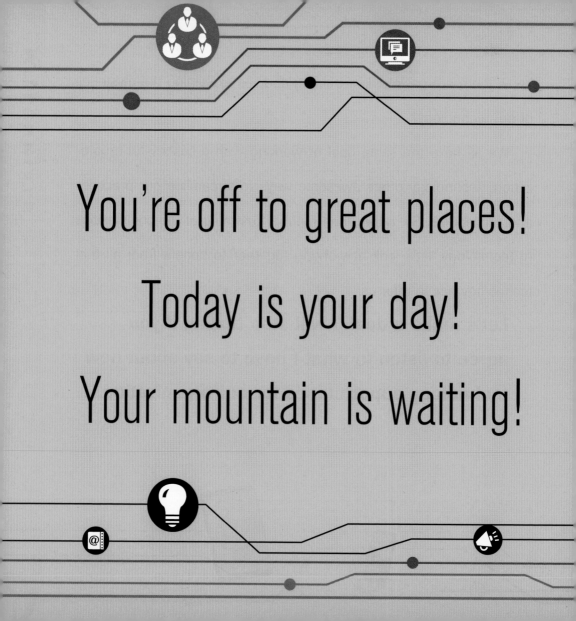

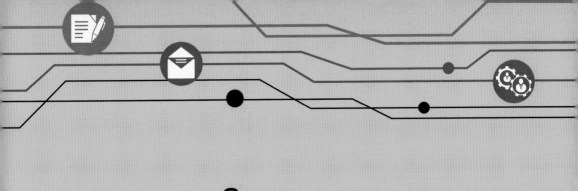

So. . .

GET ON YOUR WAY!

Dr. Seuss

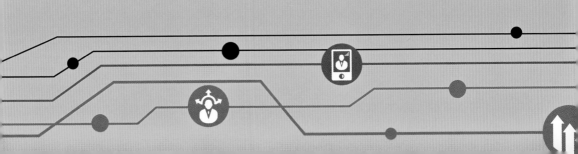

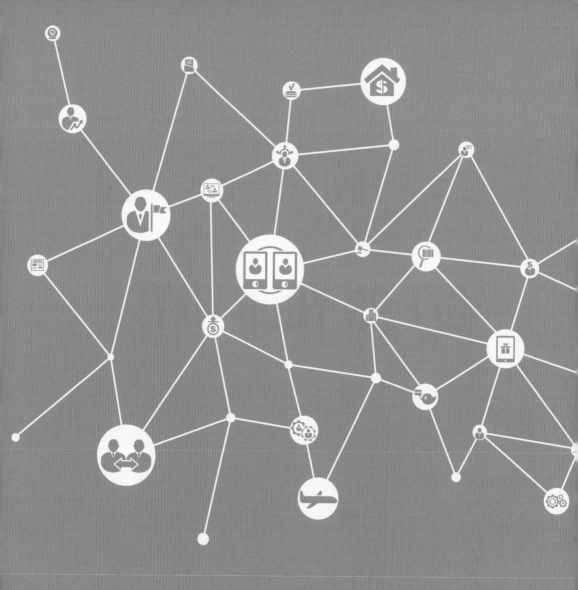

PROMOTION
AND
ADVANCEMENT

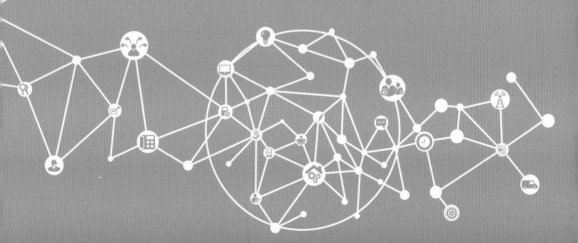

When I started in this position, my family reminded me to be grateful I even had a job. Their heartfelt instructions for the path to success were to start on the bottom rung, pay my dues by working hard, and never rock the boat. That way I'd eventually get promoted and be on my way to a fulfilling and long-lasting career with the organization.

I don't know if I like this plan at all. Why start at an entry-level position when I know as much, if not more, than people who have been here several years? If I don't know a certain skill, I can certainly learn it fast enough. I want to feel connected to this organization in a way that lets me know I can advance my career…and as quickly as possible.

Before I took this job, I spent time researching the organization. My goal was to work at a place offering room to learn, grow, and contribute. I don't want to wait for a yearly performance review before getting performance feedback and learning more about growth and advancement possibilities.

Work for me is somewhere I go and something I do in combination with other aspects of my life. I want my job to be a constantly growing and evolving factor that gives me personal satisfaction. While the paycheck is important, my larger concern is being acknowledged for the good work I do, from recognition and positive reinforcement, to personal and professional development opportunities.

Someone said Millennials are "recognition addicts." True, we're used to getting recognized for the things we do. Now that we're out in the "real" world, we assume we'll get recognition for our professional accomplishments. I do work hard, get along with my team members, volunteer for extra assignments, and get the job done. That may mean I toot my horn a bit, want special acknowledgements, and positive things to happen quickly, but that's just the way of the world for many Millennials like me.

Some of my friends found themselves stuck in dead-end jobs. They felt their hard work and effort simply never got appreciated. So they started their own businesses. Some, although not all, of those entrepreneurial start-ups are doing quite well! Instead of waiting for a chance to advance in the organization, these Millennials went ahead and created their own companies. Since not all of us can or will start our own organizations, we can all still learn from these lessons and apply them here.

Many Millennials think and function at a much faster speed than Boomers when it comes to promotion and advancement. Obviously these opportunities cannot be created out of thin air, but building a positive workplace culture encouraging personal and professional development is a very realistic outcome.

If teams and organizations today hope to recruit and retain the best and brightest employees available, then they need to build a workplace that matches the needs of high caliber Millennials.

Walk awhile in a Millennial's shoes. Never make permanent decisions on temporary feelings and emotions.

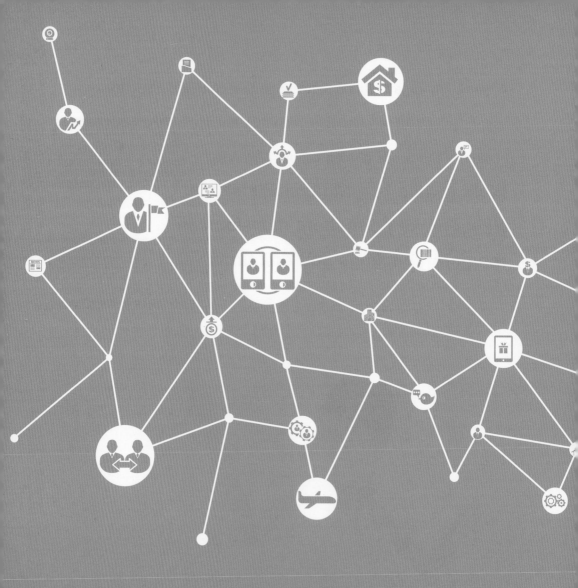

DECISION-
MAKING

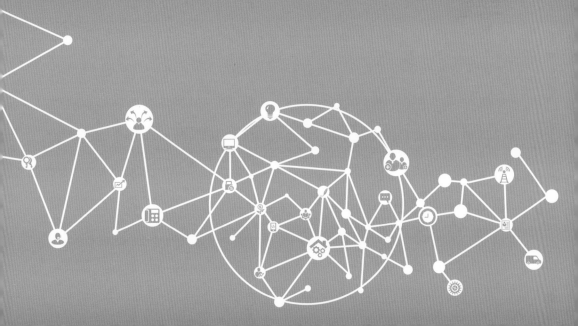

Should I live alone or with a roommate? Spend my vacation volunteering abroad or relax on the beach? Stay at a job I don't really like or start my own business? Start saving my money for the future or just use it to enjoy the present? Every day I face hundreds of decisions. They aren't just major life-changing decisions that I have to make. Even small choices end up affecting decisions I made or am about to make.

Growing up, I had plenty of people helping me with decisions. My parents would help me list the pros and cons of various choices I faced, such as what to do after high school or how to earn money to help pay for a car. In school, teachers guided me to taking various classes or applying for scholarships. It's comfortable to know mentors and people who care about you are there to help you make wise decisions. However, the older I get the more I realize the importance of making wise, personal decisions.

I admit it's easy to be paralyzed about all the decisions I have to make. I often procrastinate and then just react to whatever happens. It's fun to live in the moment and not get tied up with all the complexities of life. I like to trust my gut and make decisions based on my feelings instead of facts. Yet, realistically I know that's not the best way to handle the decision-making process. What works best for me is to get feedback from friends and family about what to consider for the decision I am pondering. My friends are the same way. They ask for advice on subjects from which car to buy to choosing a roommate. Someone called it the Distributed Problem Solving Model. That's a fancy way of saying I like people to help me with the decision-making process.

I believe that when one person makes all of the decisions it limits growth and stifles creativity for the rest of us. You know Millennials learn fast! By including us in the decision-making process, things start to happen. Ideas flow and innovations flourish! There's a certain creative flow that begins when different age groups start making decisions. A wider spectrum of ideas gets incorporated as we all see things from a different perspective. After all, decision-making should be inclusive.

You might get irritated and perplexed by how Millennials make decisions. We talk among ourselves, check some statistics on Google, and then watch a short video for more clarification on the topic. It all happens fast as a collaborative effort. Decision-making for you is more of a top-down directive. (And you may not take advantage of social media to help make your decisions.)

At work I may be asked to make decisions concerning the effectiveness of our website. Other times, I need to decide how to handle the totally rude and belligerent customer standing in front of me. Making the proper decision is crucial since each decision has a consequence. Those consequences play a part in determining the success of our organization. I don't take that lightly! Often, on-the-spot decision-making situations require me to think on my own. I have to make rational, professional decisions without the luxury of research or discussing things with my coworkers. Try to remember that while you have years of experience in making work-related decisions, I'm still learning how my decisions affect others and the organization.

Listen and share your experiences and suggestions with me so we can succeed together.

I've been there before. Let me share how I learned to handle it.

That's would be great. Let's get some coffee and chat.

MILLENNIALS vs BOOMERS

If you don't like

these rules,

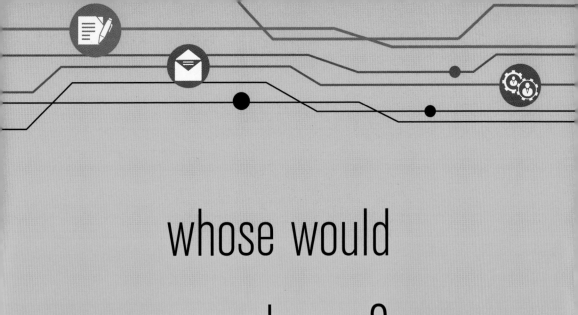

whose would

you choose?

Charlie Brown

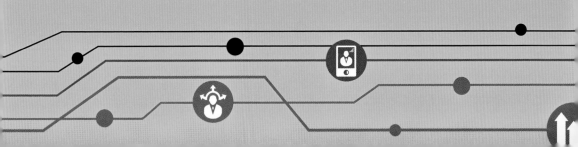

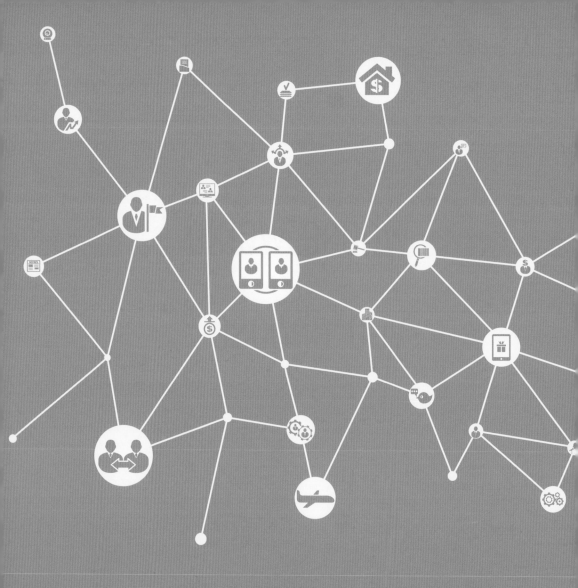

RULES
AND
REGULATIONS

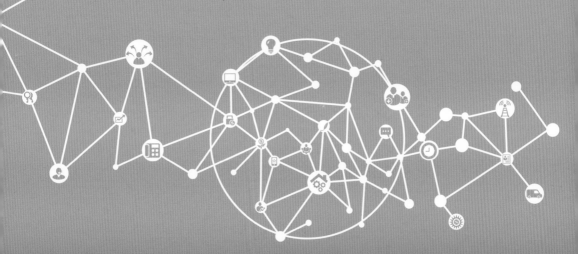

Growing up, my parents rarely gave me specific *rules.* Rather, they taught us *principles* about showing respect and taking responsibility. For example, I did not have much of a curfew or specific chores to complete. We just worked out these family issues as they came up, rather than having hard and fast rules. It worked for us!

Now I come to work and find myself facing a never-ending list of rules and regulations. Have to be at my desk by 8:00 a.m. No jeans allowed at work. Breaks limited to fifteen minutes in the morning and afternoon.

I feel as if this rule sheet is in front of me at all times:

> Rule # 1: Do this_____

> Rule # 2: Don't do this_____

> Rule # 3: Don't do this_____

> Rule #4: Do this_____

Sometimes I feel strangled! It's hard to understand how some older staff members religiously follow these rules—they are so quick to point out when I've "disobeyed" a procedure or somehow broken a rule. I certainly don't mean to do anything wrong, but sometimes it's hard to understand *why* a certain rule is implemented.

To me, it's just important that I get the job done. Does it matter if I start at 8:00 a.m. or 8:09 a.m.? Sure, some jobs mean we need to be in a certain location at a specific time to serve customers. I understand that. Then how about a little flexibility as to when we take a break?

No one is denying the need to have strict rules about things like discrimination or sexual harassment. But do we need a rule about how long I can leave my yogurt in the staff refrigerator? It's hard to understand the need for all the trivial rules I'm encountering. We're all adults, aren't we? I may not have the years of experience you do, but I do have the ability to make good decisions. Being told I have to fill out a complicated form to get time off for a dentist appointment seems like overkill. I would certainly be more engaged at work if I felt I had more freedom from what I see as unnecessary rules and regulations.

However, I do confess it's easy to spend time using my computer or phone for personal business. Sometimes I think, "I need a new backpack. I'll just spend five minutes seeing what's on sale." Pretty soon I've gone from looking at backpacks to checking out shoes I'll need if I take that backpack on a hike. Where will I hike? I start looking at some hiking websites to find a great trail. Suddenly thirty minutes have passed. Thirty

minutes that could have been spent doing actual work. While I sometimes resent being told I can't use my computer or phone for personal
use, it's probably important to let us know what is and isn't acceptable
behavior. We are addicted to technology!

It seems easier for you to accept some of our rules and regulations
because that's how most organizations have always operated. You
start a job, get a handbook, and start following those outlined rules.
I'm more inclined to want to know "why" a certain rule is in operation.
**Because many rules are not clearly black and
white, let's review them and see which would
be better as decision-making guidelines.**

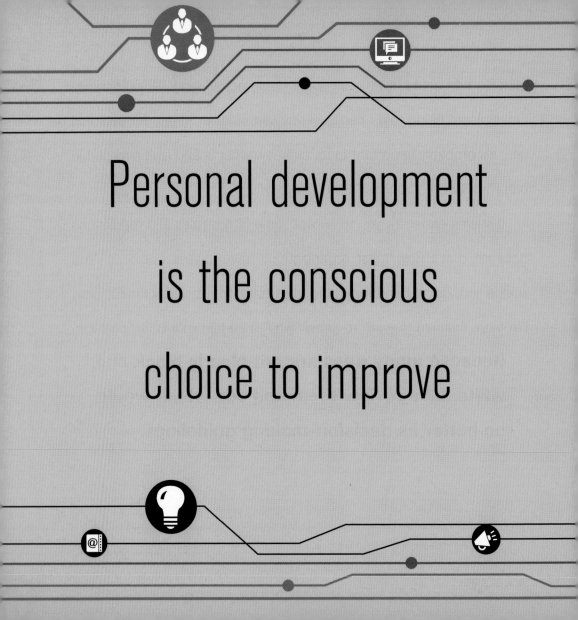

Personal development

is the conscious

choice to improve

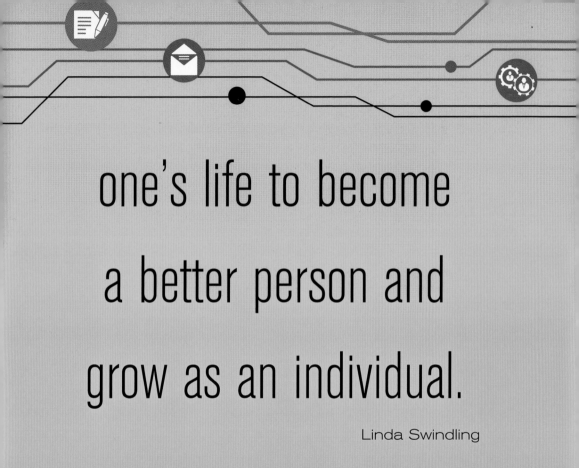

one's life to become

a better person and

grow as an individual.

Linda Swindling

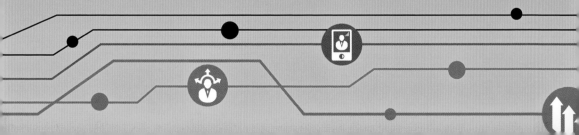

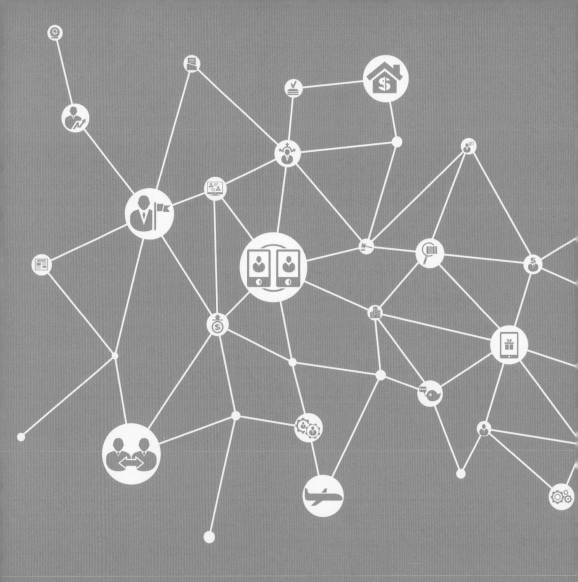

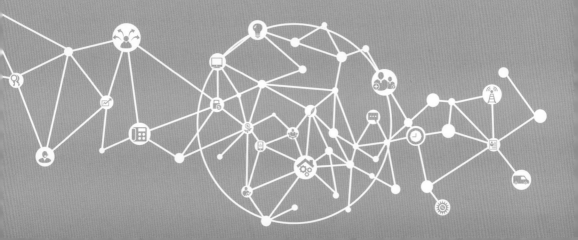

PERSONAL GROWTH AND DEVELOPMENT

f I took a personality test I'm sure I'd score high on the self-confidence scale. Why shouldn't I have faith in myself? I grew up with family, adult friends, and teachers constantly telling me great things about myself. They instilled in me that I was not only great, but also the smartest, best looking, funniest, and most creative kid in the universe. (Never mind that my friends heard the same thing from their parents.) I was told I could do anything or be anyone as long as I gave it hard work and effort.

Now, I'm not so sure that is the way the world works. I'm seeing now that my parents may have gone overboard in their exuberance for telling me just how incredible I was. (OK, my mom *still* tells me this!) As we begin our careers, we often get assigned repetitive and mundane tasks. How could such amazingly brilliant people be expected to work at entry-level jobs? That's okay. I understand we need to prove ourselves. There just seems to be a disconnect between wanting to use our talents and ending up regulated to a boring job. I want to feel challenged in what I do at work. I studied hard in school. Now my skills aren't being fully utilized. I'm ready and willing to expand my personal growth by learning new skills to help move the organization forward. While I know that I possess many strengths, at the same time I recognize I could benefit from additional training or mentoring (including from you and your Boomer buddies).

Personal growth means I'm looking for ways to better myself and learn new things. This involves changing and growing to become a more effective contributor. I want to get advancement opportunities, take the lead, and expand my responsibilities. But just because I want to grow and develop doesn't mean I always know how to. Do you want me to show initiative by suggesting new ideas, or take greater ownership of a specific area of my responsibility? I want to understand what I need to do to succeed and I will work to hit those goals. Can you help me?

It's true. Sometimes I just want to come to work, do my job, and clock out at 5:30 p.m. Sometimes I'm simply trying to get a paycheck and don't care about expanding my role or advancing my career. I would never admit this to you because I know that's not what you want to hear. But even when I'm not the most motivated person on the team, I still value my work and *am* taking my job seriously, even if it's not my long-term dream job.

Outside of work, it's also important that we better ourselves. That's why so many of us try new things like hot yoga, golf, blogging, or learning Mandarin. We can only find happiness and contentment within ourselves. There's a personal satisfaction in knowing I'm developing my personal talents and skills. When I attend a seminar or watch a TED Talk video, I'm motivated to use what I learned to advance myself at work. I discover my inner strength, which helps me understand other people's point of views. Your idea of personal development may be different from mine. As long as we each, in our own way, try to achieve positive personal growth, we'll be successful. Learning can be hard but rewarding and very beneficial at the same time.

With patience and understanding, we can learn and grow together.

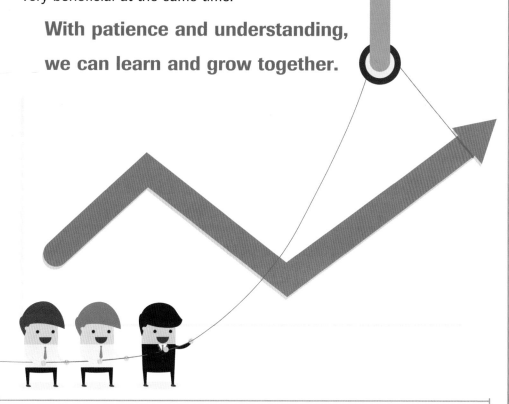

Coming together
is a beginning;
keeping together
is progress;

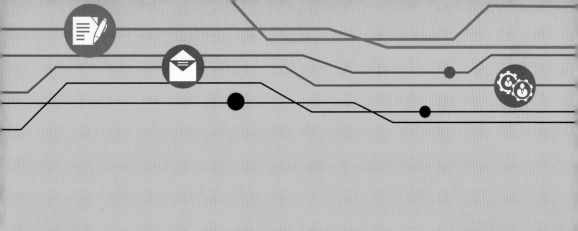

WORKING TOGETHER

IS SUCCESS.

Henry Ford

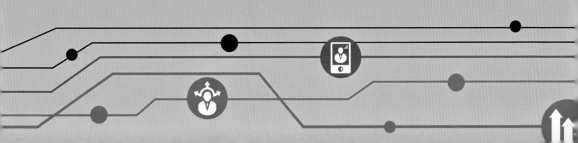

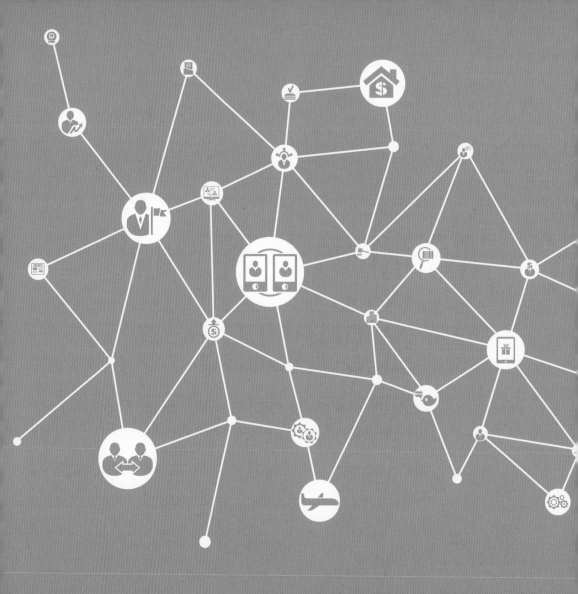

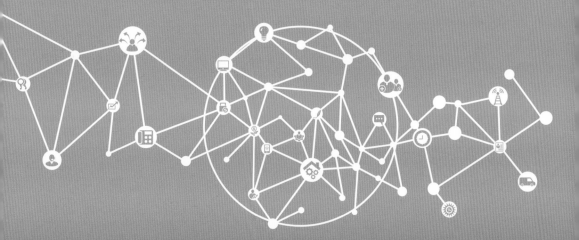

WHAT ARE THESE MESSAGES REALLY ABOUT?

Before you assume this book and my shared viewpoints are nothing more than a list of gripes and "woe is me" complaints, let me be clear. They are, in fact, just the opposite. My goal here is not only to set the record straight, but also to use this shared information to build more understanding, support, and acceptance with you and your Boomer coworkers.

Having diverse viewpoints can make the workplace more enjoyable and enriching, plus more rewarding and productive. We work in an organization with important objectives, and it's up to us to work together effectively to meet and exceed those goals.

My hope is by sharing my feelings and background information on these important workplace viewpoints, it will lead to even more appreciation and collaboration between my Millennial cohorts and your Boomer buddies.

On the future

My excitement about the future stems mostly from the hope that will produce many more opportunities for both of us to advance, grow, and achieve the personal fulfillment we all seek. My anxiety comes from the simple fear of the unknown. It comes from a deep concern that I may not be able to respond to all the changes that are happening in business today. Some, like technology changes, may be easy for me to embrace and implement. Others, like blending old-school ideas with the requirements necessary to function in today's ever-changing business environment, may be challenging for me and other Millennials

Do I have all the answers? **No.** In fact, I often have more questions than answers. However, I do know this: Yesterday is gone. The future is what we both have to work with, and the future begins today!

Anxious about the future? Just know you are not alone.

What I ask of you:

- Appreciate the fact that my challenges are no easier than yours and my viewpoints are not absolutely wrong and yours absolutely right—they're just different.
- Don't assume I am in a "my way or the highway" operational mode and unable or unwilling to make accommodations.
- Continue to challenge attitudes and behaviors, including mine, that can be enhanced and improved.
- Adopt the mind-set that for you to be successful at work, you need me as much as I need you.
- Assume half the responsibility for our working relationship. If

we make improvements together, take half the credit. If we don't make improvements, accept half the responsibility for making it better.

And when you do, I believe you will find…
With more understanding
And greater appreciation
We can meet in the middle
And succeed together.

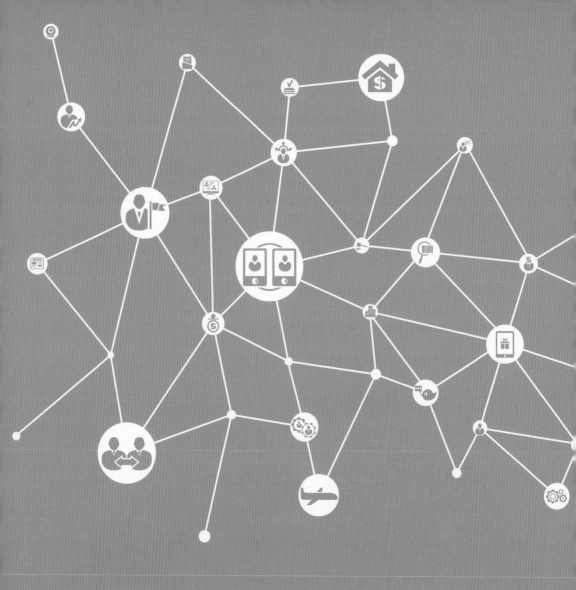

ABOUT THE AUTHORS

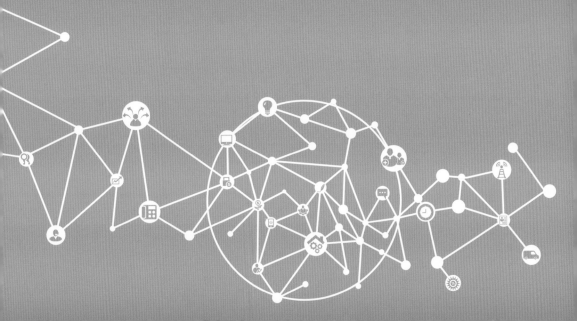

Eric Harvey is founder and president of the Walk the Talk Company and a leading expert on high-achieving leaders and organizations. Since its founding in 1977, Walk the Talk has worked with thousands of organizations worldwide, including multinational corporations, leading health care providers, high-tech start-ups, and highly respected nonprofit organizations. Eric has authored twenty-five books that have sold millions of copies including the bestsellers *Walk the Talk, Ethics 4 Everyone, Walk Awhile in My Shoes*, and *Go for the Gold*. He and his wife, Nancy, live in Pensacola Beach, Florida, and are the proud parents of two daughters and have six grandchildren.

Silvana Clark spent six weeks living with 120 Millennials to start her research for this book. Before that, she wrote twelve books, carried the torch for the 2012 Olympics (not for her athletic prowess!), appeared on Fox's *Trading Spouses*, and spent nineteen months living and working from a branded RV. A professional speaker, Silvana travels the country giving motivational keynotes and presentations on how businesses can benefit from harnessing the energy and skills of Millennials.

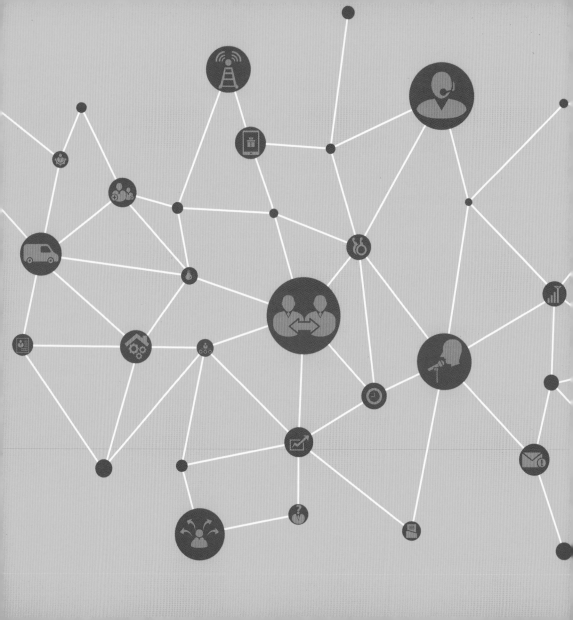

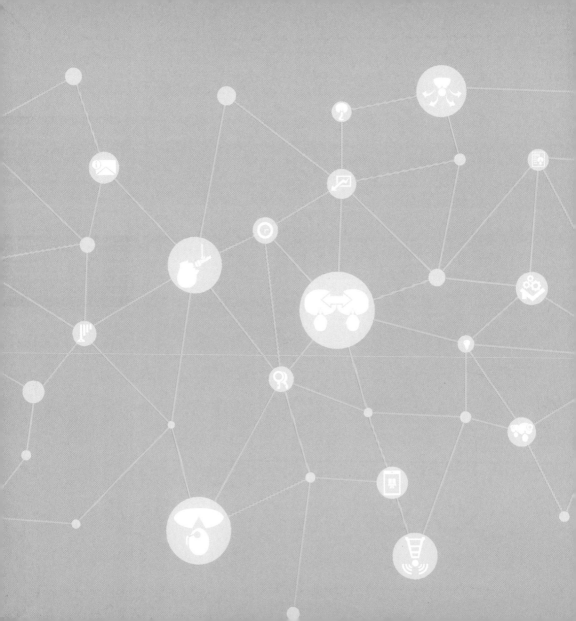

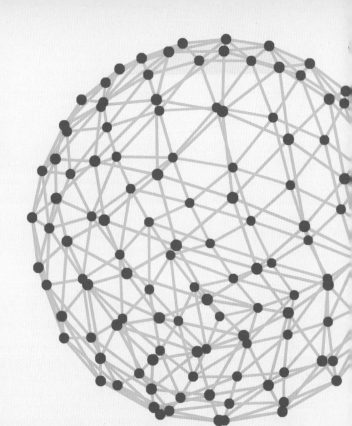

simple ▶ truths®
small books, BIG IMPACT.

Eric Harvey & Silvana Clark

Listen, learn, and SUCCEED Together

BOOMERS VS. MILLENNIALS

Photo Credits
Cover: AntartStock/Shutterstock
Internals: page 1 AntartStock/Shutterstock; pages 8–9, phipatbig/Shutterstock, Creative-idea/iStock; pages 10–11, teerayut tae/Shutterstock; pages 29, 45, 61, 69, 77, 83, 91, 99, 107, Ingka D. Jiw/Shutterstock.

Published by Simple Truths, an imprint of Sourcebooks, Inc.
P.O. Box 4410, Naperville, Illinois 60567-4410
(630) 961-3900
Fax: (630) 961-2168
www.sourcebooks.com

Printed and bound in China.

QL 10 9 8 7 6 5 4 3 2

Managing multigenerational workforces is an art in itself. Young workers want to make a quick impact, the middle generation needs to believe in the mission, and older employees don't like ambivalence. Your move.

Harvard Business School

BOOMERS
VS.
MILLENNIALS

Listen, Learn, and Succeed Together

n today's workplace we often have a coworker population that can represent age gaps of forty-plus years. With that range comes a host of different experiences, expectations, and perspectives. *Boomers vs. Millennials* will give readers a better understanding and appreciation of viewpoint differences in these important workplace areas:

BOOMERS vs MILLENNIALS

This powerful resource represents workplace viewpoints from two perspectives. One side will cover the experiences and attitudes of our "seasoned" employees, aka Baby Boomers, while the other side of the book covers the perspectives of your newer and younger employees, aka Millennials.

Boomers vs. Millennials is designed to bridge perception differences and viewpoint gaps. This book is designed to help you create more understanding and acceptance of ideas, while ensuring more success for individuals, work teams, and the entire organization.

Dear Millennial,

We are every person you deal with that was born between 1946 and 1964. We are affectionately known as Baby Boomers, and we represent a significant population of people you work with every day. Some of us are your team members, some are your managers, and some are reporting directly to you.

We may have different sizes, shapes, colors, beliefs, and experiences. We are older and more "seasoned" than you and your contemporaries. Our age differences can and do cause different viewpoints to naturally occur. Neither of us is typically absolutely right and the other absolutely wrong, but our perspectives may be quite different. Those differences can become strengths or weakness depending on how they are appreciated and how they are managed.

Just like you and your fellow Millennials, I want to be understood, accepted, and appreciated for what I have contributed. For that to occur, we both need to do a better job of understanding and appreciating our different viewpoints.

The following pages are about opening up to you—about sharing my feelings on many aspects of my job and working with you. This new information, I hope, will encourage you to see me in a new, and perhaps different, light.

Please listen to these messages with the same level of compassion and understanding that you wish from me as I read the flip side of this book. Chances are we will both discover new insights about our respective viewpoints that enable us to meet in the middle and succeed together.

Many ideas grow better when transplanted into another

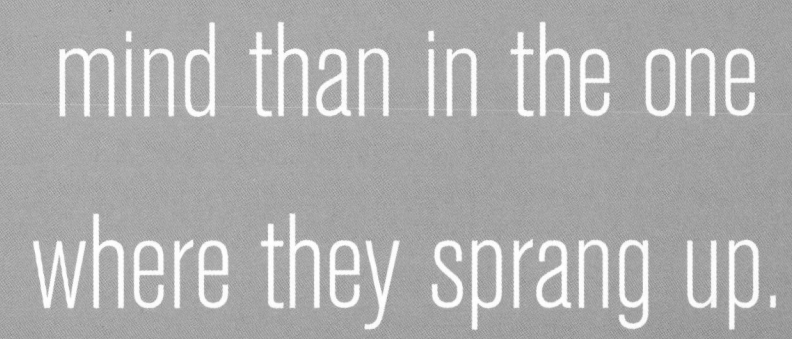

mind than in the one
where they sprang up.

Oliver Wendell Holmes

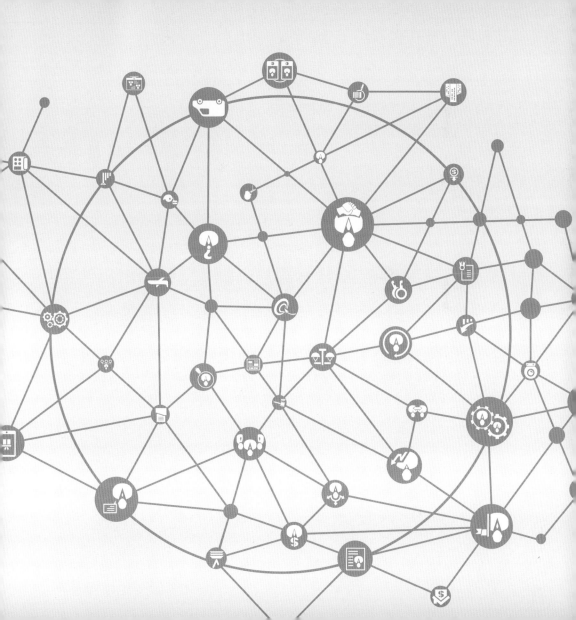

TEAMWORK
AND
WORKING
TOGETHER

Talent wins games, but teamwork and intelligence win championships.

Michael Jordan

While working my way up the organizational ladder, it was easy to become a "lone wolf." Sure, I collaborated with some people on certain work activities, but basically I did my job without having to run every idea past members of my team. There was a boss and there were worker bees. Few people had time (or saw the need) to continuously get together to share ideas or ask for input on every project. Most of us had individual jobs to do, so there did not seem to be a need to have multiple staff meetings.

Now I'm working more and more with younger staff members on team projects, and that takes some learning on my part. Because of my

history, I am more accustomed to team members independently working on their own set of objectives and tasks.

In addition to my challenges concerning team decision-making, I also get annoyed with some of your information gathering techniques. In meetings, for example, it's very frustrating for me to discover that half of you are texting while the other half are Googling for information. Based on my past experiences it's hard for me to not see these habits as technological distractions. I understand your skill sets and ways of doing business are different than mine, which is why it is so important for us to fully agree and understand our goals and common objectives. With that clarity I will be much more willing to accept different ways and techniques to achieve those important outcomes.

I see you enjoy the camaraderie that comes with working together in groups. Also, like you, I understand the benefits of getting contributions

from many sources. However, we all need to remember that working as a team involves more than just being assigned a task and getting the opportunity to work with other people. Ultimately it means producing important results.

I read a parable about some animals that wanted to start a school. They decided all animals had to take classes in swimming, flying, climbing, and running. Naturally the rabbit and cheetah were great at running, but they couldn't keep up with the ducks and fish when it came to swimming. It took a while for the animals to realize they all had unique abilities. Hopefully it won't take us long to realize the value in recognizing the unique skill sets we all have as individual team members.

Having an abundance of work experiences under my belt, I realize it's my responsibility to help create an environment where everyone feels valued and knows they are a vital part of our organization. So, let's

brainstorm ways we can create a cohesive team by emphasizing our individual strengths.

I see now that the problem-solving skills we learn from working as a team can help us accomplish goals and overcome communication barriers. We may not always have all the same ideas, but a well-run team creates an atmosphere where everyone feels respected enough to share their thoughts and opinions. By listening and learning from the experience of others, we create a productive team. This also creates a collaborative work environment where we all benefit.

When we learn from our individual talents and work as a team, there is no limit to our potential achievements.

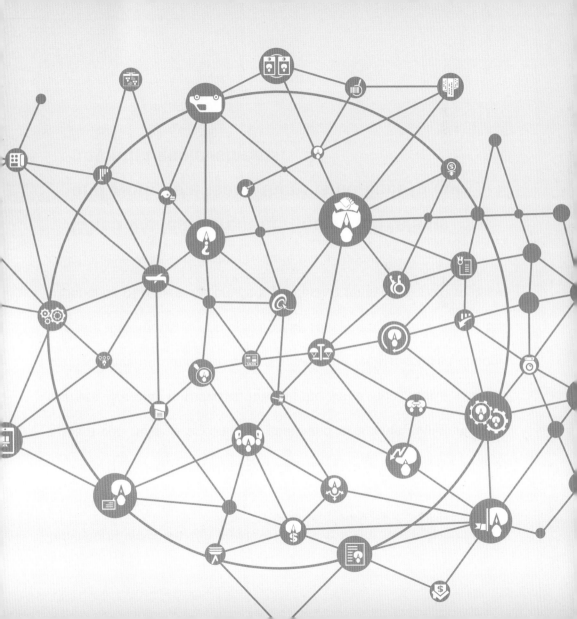

LOYALTY TO THE JOB AND THE ORGANIZATION

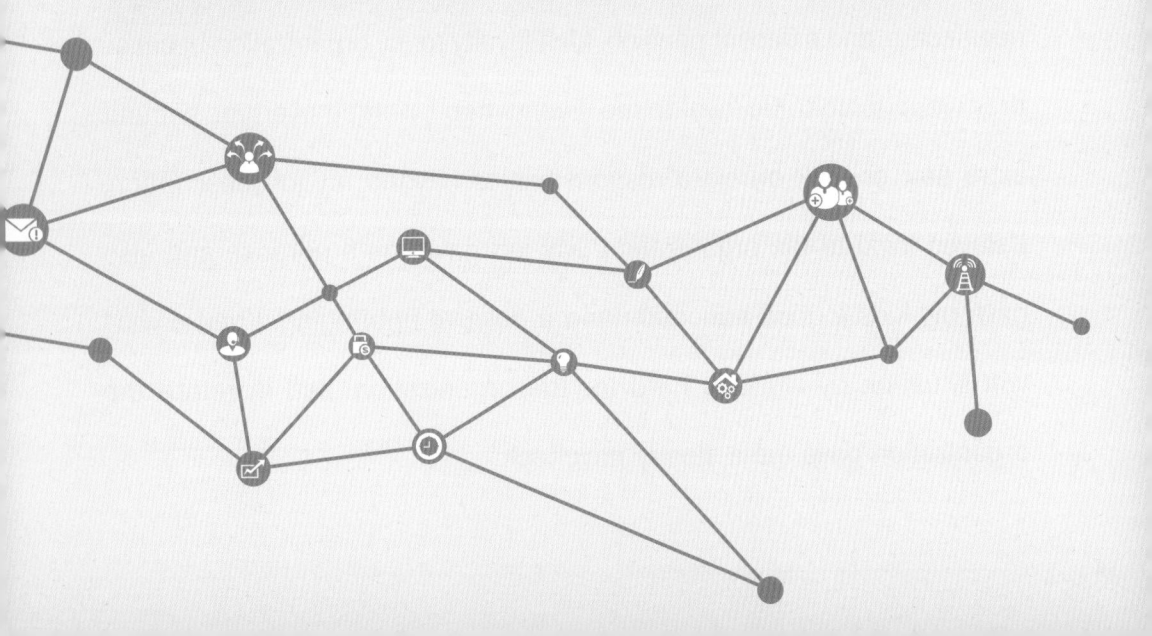

You give loyalty, you'll get it back.

Tommy Lasorda

T hings aren't like they used to be!

When I started working in an entry-level position, I assumed I'd be rewarded for my hard work with long-term employment, health care, and a decent pension. I felt loyalty to my organization because they were going to be loyal to me. Even when I worked overtime without extra pay, or took on extra responsibilities beyond my job description, I stayed loyal to the organization. My job gave me a purpose and also gave my kids a good education and a positive upbringing. I had a win-win situation by working hard for the organization, and in return the organization gave me a steady paycheck.

Now I see the work environment changing. Today we find more organizational restructuring and layoffs. Let's not forget the downsizing! Wait—we're not being downsized; we're being "right-sized." No matter what you call it, some long-term employees are finding themselves as middle-aged job seekers. Younger employees often don't feel the same need to be loyal because it's easier for them to change jobs, even if it means moving across the country.

With an established lifestyle, I have to think long and hard about what it would mean to change jobs. That might involve uprooting my family, selling our house, and leaving friends and loved ones. Younger employees, with fewer considerations like this, can often make these decisions much faster and easier.

While I continue to stay loyal, I often resent that my experience and knowledge about the business do not seem to count for as much as they

used to. Sure, I may not be a whiz with technology like most Millennials, but I'm certainly willing to learn. What I lack in technology skills I make up for with institutional knowledge and market experience.

Loyalty is definitely a two-way street. When I see people trying to implement changes in a considerate and professional way, they have my loyalty. I understand that when times are hard we can't have huge raises and may not have 100-percent-paid health benefits. But I'll tell you one thing: my loyalty definitely increases when I'm recognized for my accomplishments. I also benefit from seeing that we have positive, productive leaders running our organization.

Loyalty means different things to different people. Some people are loyal to the job because they have flexible hours. Others are loyal because they are assured a yearly cost-of-living raise. Some employees develop loyalty to an organization when they get to go to conferences

and receive additional training. When it comes to demonstrating my loyalty, I recognize that part of my job as a seasoned member of our organization is helping you grow, learn, and develop more commitment to your job. You may not see your position as a lifelong career choice, but it's helpful to feel loyalty to the job, even if it is short-term.

Since I value being recognized, I want to look for more ways to let you know that you're also an asset to our team and this organization. You have talents and knowledge that benefit all of us. Often work loyalty is related to job relationships. By communicating with you more often, and trusting your decision-making ability, loyalty for both of us will increase.

Creating loyalty at work requires a trusting relationship. So let's work together to make that happen.

If you don't like
something, change it.

If you can't change it,
change your attitude.

Maya Angelou

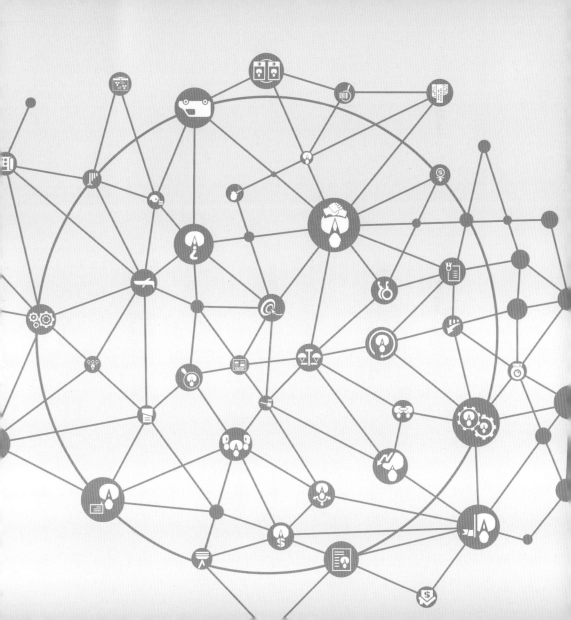

DEALING
WITH
CHANGE

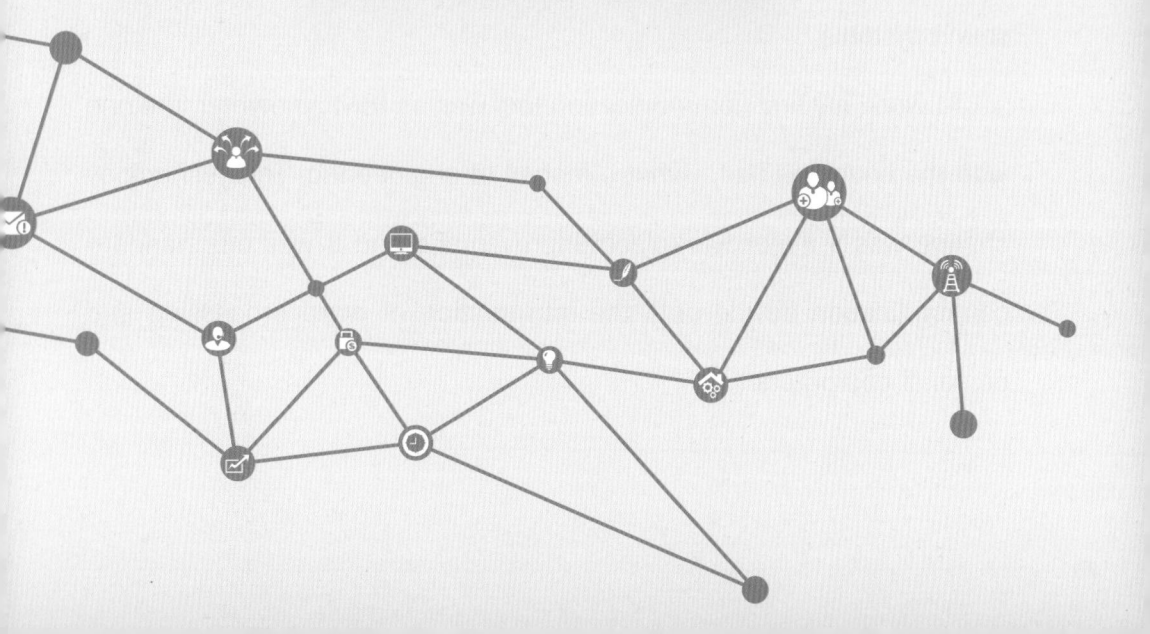

P robably no workplace situation is more challenging to me than dealing with change. It's not that I inherently resist change, because I don't. My challenges are more about the speed of change.

Growing up, my family got our first color television when I was in middle school, and that wonderful piece of technology stayed in our living room for many years. In addition, that TV became the standard for home entertainment until the introduction of flat-screens and multimedia sound systems.

At work, my first communication tool was an IBM typewriter, the one with the bouncing ball…what a marvel of engineering. This technology change was a major workplace improvement, and it was our standard communication device until the introduction of word processing and personal computers.

Today, things continue to change at an increasingly rapid pace. We have changes in technology, practices, decision-making, workforce composition, the goods and services we provide, etc. I truly understand these changes are important and necessary for **many** reasons. However, these changes sometimes require some relearning and reconditioning on my part and for some of my Boomer buddies.

Change can be a diametrically opposed phenomenon for many Boomers. On one hand, we understand that change is necessary to maintain our personal significance as well as to ensure the viability of our organization. On the other hand, change can sometimes be downright scary! What if we make the wrong change, support the wrong technology, can't change fast enough, or are just incapable of adjusting to the new world order? Does that mean we are no longer relevant and therefore no longer needed?

In addition to speed, another significant challenge of change is the personal feeling of **being** changed…which I'm sure is a challenge for you as well. New ideas and ways of doing business are essential, but there are techniques we can use to ensure that change is less resisted and fully supported.

I believe it is essential to develop everyone's understanding about the "hows" of change and even more importantly the "whys." We're all big boys and girls and we need that meaningful information.

So, bottom line, am I an opponent of change? No, not at all! In fact, when you look at our history growing up in the '60s and '70s, older Boomers went through some major social and political changes and came out even smarter and more resilient in the process. Boomers have the skills and experiences to do the same going forward as long as you

keep us informed, involved, and consider us as collaborators instead of obstacles.

Change is something we all need to embrace, and Boomers want to be your change partners.

To effectively communicate, we must realize that we are all different in the way we perceive the

world and use this under-

standing as a guide to our

communication with others.

Anthony Robbins

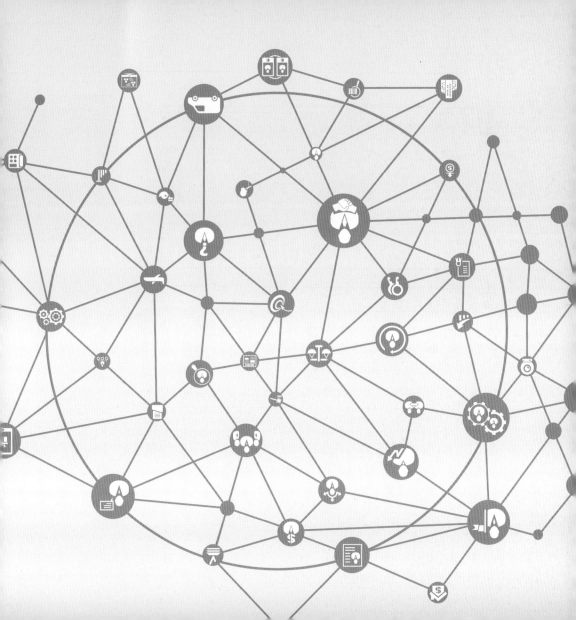

THE QUALITY AND QUANTITY OF COMMUNICATION

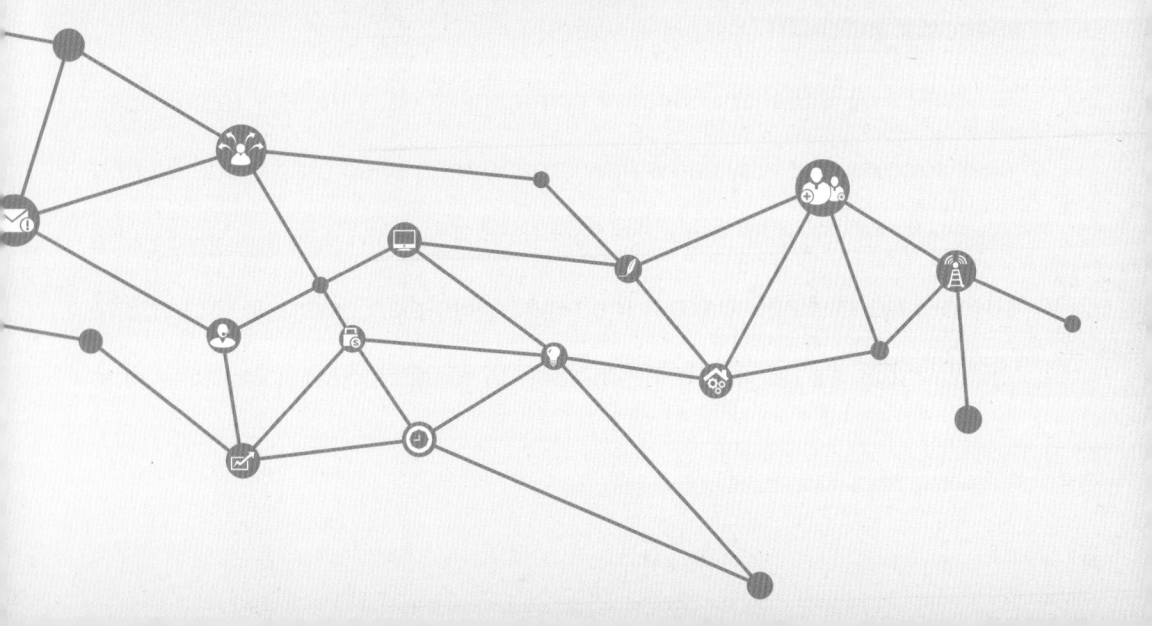

When I was taking a business communication class in college, we spent an entire week learning to write a proper internal business memo. There were rules about style, content, punctuation, grammar, format, and spelling. When we turned in a paper, the teacher lowered our grade if there were misspelled words. We didn't have spell-check! Now I'm expected to communicate with you quickly and simply using 140 characters or less. (At least it doesn't matter as much if I misspell a word!)

Here's my situation: Effective communication is the key to our business success. Yet how can a new organization-wide dress code be fully explained to you with a tweet? Last month our organization sent out a seven-page document about the new health plan coverage, but you've told me that it's too much information to read. However, you take time

at our staff meeting to ask questions about the health plan that were clearly outlined in the report that we all received.

When we have weekly staff meetings to go over major work-related topics, I see you getting antsy and trying to sneak peeks at your phone. Communicating with email, social media, and quick chats in meetings are ways to touch base about business issues under certain circumstances, but on other occasions we need to communicate with more detailed written material and longer face-to-face conversations. No one enjoys long meetings, especially when they consist of dull and repetitive topics. As we both know, not all communication can be quick and entertaining. However, it is important to not only be respectful with the communication strategies you choose, but also select the right technique for the right time and purpose.

Like you, I want to improve communication in our organization, so I'm going to make an extra effort to communicate with you in a more effective fashion. Maybe that means taking the time to introduce you to a new coworker. Would you like to sit in on a staff meeting you normally don't attend? If I communicate with you in different ways, you'll be more aware of what is happening in our organization. You'll understand the overall picture of what we do and why it is done that way. In return, I'd like your full attention, although I know you are excellent at multitasking.

When it comes to face-to-face communication, I'm trying to find a balance between being businesslike and being friendly. My door is open (most of the time), so you can feel free to discuss work-related issues with me. If I don't have time at that particular minute to talk with you, let's set up a time to talk when we're both free. Please understand that,

like you, I'm busy with many projects so my availability needs to be taken into consideration.

I fully realize that effective communication is the key to developing successful relationships and accomplishing important business goals. I commit to try to do my very best to break down communication barriers we might have and I ask the same of you. With that agreement we can all do a better job of listening, learning, and working more effectively.

Intelligence, knowledge, and experience are important, but strong communication skills are how we build positive relationships and get big things done.

A true balance between work and life comes with knowing

that your life activities are
integrated not separated.

Michael Thomas Sunnarborg

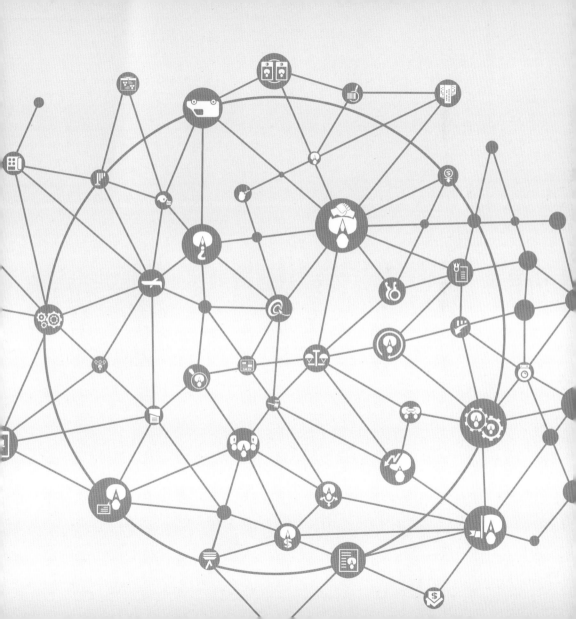

WORK-LIFE BALANCE

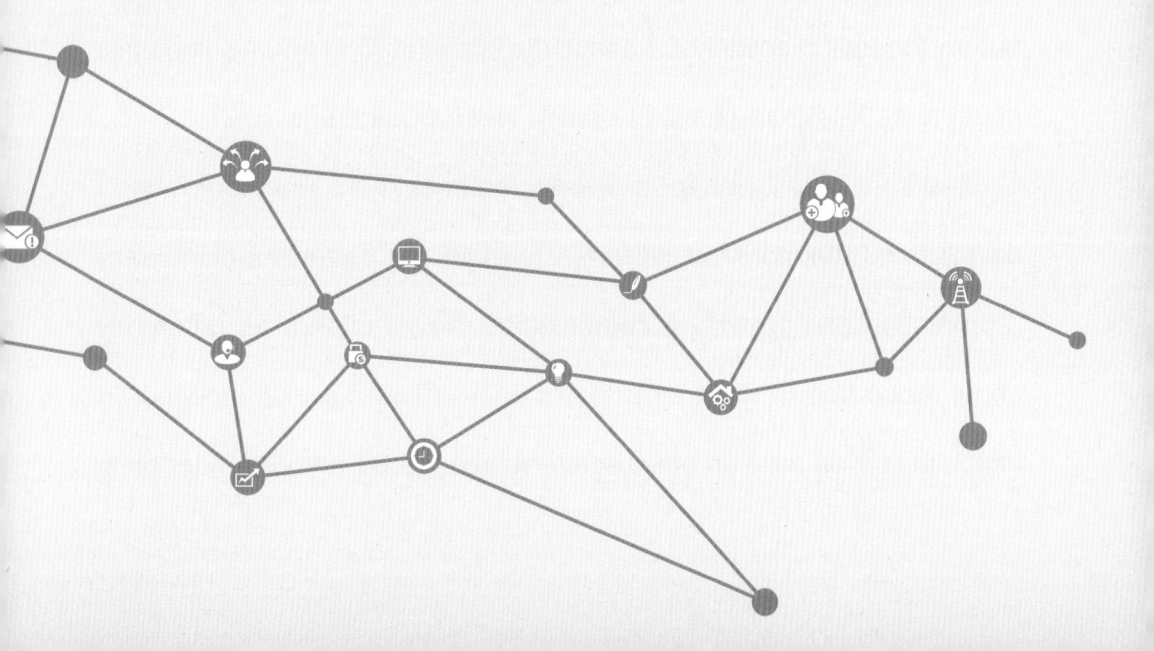

Getting my first job with a decent salary and basic benefits made a big impact on my life. I was finally grown-up! Now I needed to devote my time and effort to doing all I could to be the best employee possible. That meant working long hours, coming in on occasional weekends, and never saying no to additional work. My gut kept saying, "Keep on working!" "Don't take a sick day!" "Offer to take on additional responsibilities!" I missed some of my kid's special events, but my job took precedence. I admit, the stressful, long hours sometimes made me a less-than-pleasant person when I was home.

That's the way it was in the workforce back then. The more hours I devoted and the more special projects I had, the better the chance for a promotion and possibly a corner office. Now I think a bit differently about those things. Regarding that corner office? Never happened! In fact, I don't even have an office since we changed to an open-floor plan.

There's an ingrained desire in me to give all I can to an employer that helps me provide a good life for my family and myself. My family and I had the resources we needed to provide for our kids, and along the way, we took some fun vacations. (Although my family did occasionally complain about how often I checked in with work when I should have been in the pool playing Marco Polo with the kids.)

When meeting new people, I always introduced myself with my name and occupation. It didn't matter that I had outside skills and interests or desires to write a book or learn to scuba dive. It was my job that defined who I was. Now I'm beginning to understand the critical importance of work-life balance and am starting to accept the concept more each day. It takes effort to leave work at a reasonable hour or even take time to invite a friend to a nonwork lunch. I work hard during regular work

work hours, so I shouldn't feel bad if I leave a little early, to watch my daughter's high school volleyball game.

Now I'm slowly seeing the need to not only have more enjoyment at work, but also to not let work consume my life. After watching how you and your Millennial colleagues seem to better achieve balance in your personal and professional lives, I'm glad to listen and learn from you and your cohorts. In addition, I am especially impressed with how millennial men appear to have more positive attitudes toward female coworkers and a more egalitarian perspective on pay, performance, contributions, and work-life balance. Millennial men want to be home for their daughters' volleyball games too.

Please remember, dear colleagues, that my early job experiences have influenced my current viewpoints about work-life balance. Every day I see the personal benefits of your expectations, and I am trying to grow

into your way of thinking on this and many other varying viewpoints we may have.

However, change in people and in organizations does not come overnight. So the next time you have some ideas about how we can get better work-life balance at work, please share them with me and my Boomer buddies.

Let's listen, learn, and look for more effective work-life balance solutions together.

Working together is more than a good idea,

it's essential to individual
and organizational success.

Sondra Thiederman

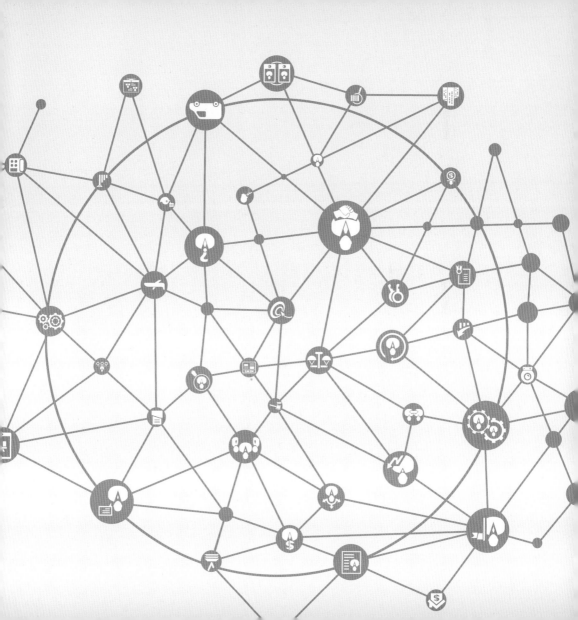

DIVERSITY AND INCLUSION

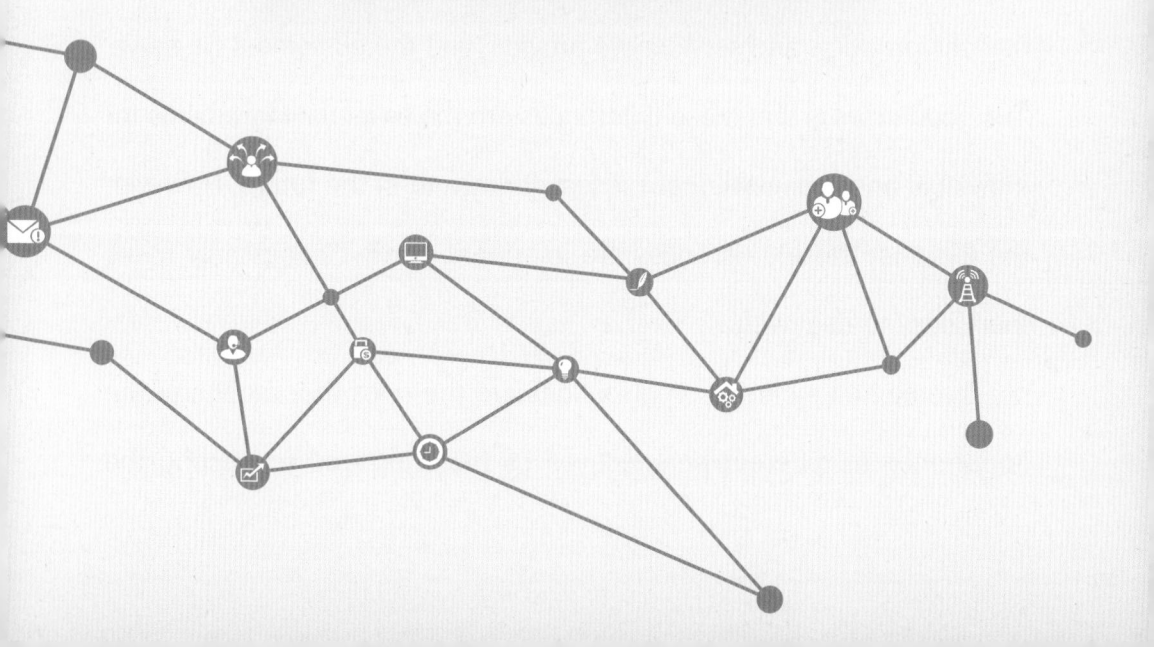

OK, let's talk about diversity from a seasoned Boomer's perspective: We had one black-and-white TV in the living room with three channels. We had one dog, one car, Dad went to work, Mom stayed home, and you got a job after graduation and stayed there until retirement. That was diversity!

Today diversity is a **much** bigger topic, and it is much more than race, gender, and ethnic differences. We have differences in the technology we use, the products and services we provide, and the customers we serve. The good news is that these differences are the essential ingredients for individual and organizational success today and in the future. However, the fact that these differences are important doesn't necessarily make them easy to deal with.

Diverse and inclusive organizations are the ones that recognize the importance of different perspectives by honoring and respecting the

ideas and efforts of every individual. Again, I must admit, those realities are sometimes challenging for us Boomers. It's often easier for us to wish the way things used to be would return…but we clearly know they won't, and in fact, they shouldn't!

So, when it comes to diversity and inclusion, I see it as a two-way street and an opportunity to work together. We all have a shared stake in the success of our organization, so all of us have a responsibility to respond to and capitalize on today's diverse population of people and their diverse perspectives. Ultimately we need to turn these realities into inclusive and successful outcomes—and do that better than our competition!

For example we need to recognize that:

- A diverse and inclusive workforce opens doors to a more expanded and diverse customer base.

- A diverse and inclusive workplace produces new and more effective decisions, products, and services.

- A diverse and inclusive workplace breaks down counterproductive "we vs. they" attitudes and behaviors.

- A diverse and inclusive workplace enables us to recruit and retain the best and brightest people.

Boomers with awareness clearly know that diversity and inclusion are essential for personal and professional success. We are trying to fully understand and accept all the differences that have occurred

in the workplace over these past thirty to forty years. But again, that understanding for some is not necessarily easy.

As I write these words I am even more aware of my responsibility to be a driver of diversity and inclusion and not just sit back and talk about the good old days. Which, I might add, were **not** so good for a **lot** of people!

As we and our organization continue to become more diverse and inclusive, please remember what it was like for us Boomers when we started our careers. That is not an excuse, just a perspective we ask you to take into consideration.

Next time you are thinking about Boomers

in regard to diversity…

walk awhile in our shoes.

But enough about me...

What do you think of me?

Bette Midler

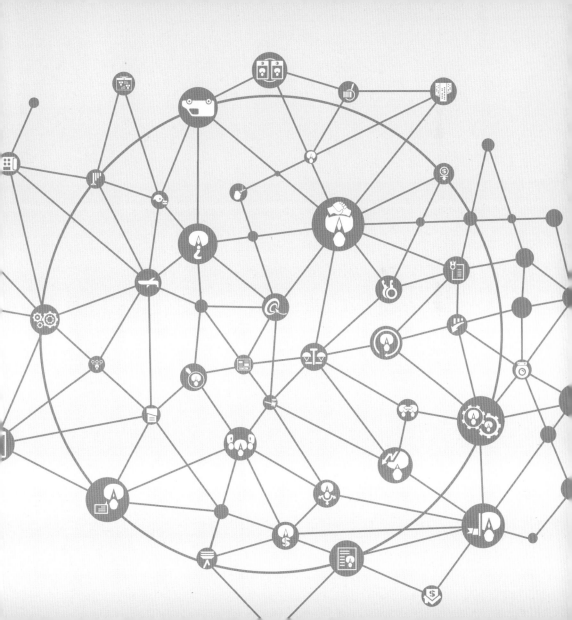

REWARDS
AND
RECOGNITION

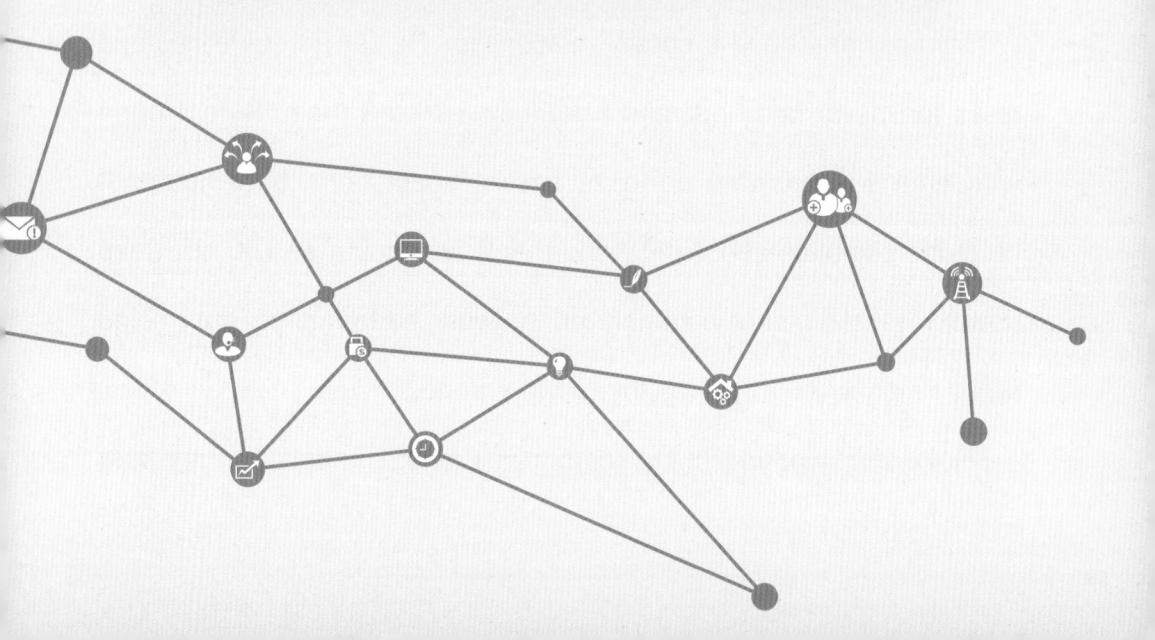

remember when I was hired at my first "real" job many years ago. I met with coworkers and proudly wore my organization's ID card attached to a colorful lanyard. Then I admired my bulky desktop computer… complete with floppy disks. Making a good impression was very important, and I certainly didn't want to rock the boat in any way. I listened at staff meetings and tried to pick up the culture of the organization so I would fit in with the rest of the staff.

My boss and I had a cordial relationship. He set up guidelines and tasks for me to carry out and I dutifully followed them. Sure, I often wondered if I was living up to my boss's expectations, but I figured if he didn't complain about my work, then I was doing an OK job. Deep down, I wanted him to comment on my work performance, but I could see it simply wasn't the way things were done.

Now, after working many years in my field, I understand my boss

didn't have time to comment on every project I completed or notice every time I stayed late to help a customer. Unfortunately, today's fast-paced world may not always allow us to meet on a regular schedule and not all accomplishments may be able to be acknowledged. This does not mean that I am not aware or appreciative of your hard work and all that you do for our team.

While I do see and hear positive things about team members, I may not always comment on or immediately acknowledge them. And, if I am being honest here, there is an "old-school" part of me that believes recognition for just doing the job that you're supposed to do is unnecessary. You met with three new clients? Updated the organization's LinkedIn page? Calmed an angry customer? If those tasks were standard and expected it means you're simply doing your job.

Just because work used to be a place to get down to "serious

business" doesn't mean it has to be that way today. It's important I start looking for ways to "pat you on the back," figuratively and literally. Who doesn't like to be recognized for something they've accomplished? How can I make you feel more valued? We all want our efforts to be noticed. Not with a ticker-tape parade (that would be fun, wouldn't it?) but with small actions. Sometimes a simple thank-you or a quick text is all it takes. I'll try to do that more often.

The Great Places to Work Institute conducts research on the importance of workplace enjoyment and recognition at work. Their research demonstrates how positive reinforcement correlates to positive performance. People working at organizations where they feel rewarded and acknowledged form better relationships with coworkers, customers, and produce better results. Isn't that what we all want?

Perhaps all of us could acknowledge each other more. When you see someone going above their normal duties, let them know you noticed. Also, be sure to tell a coworker you overheard a customer making a positive statement about his or her performance. In other words, look for opportunities to catch people doing something right!

By acknowledging others they in turn, will more than likely acknowledge you. In this way, we all get the recognition that makes us feel valued!

I really enjoyed working with you on that project. You did a great job! Thank you!

BOOMERS VS MILLENNIALS

Life was much simpler

when Apple and

Blackberry were simply fruits.

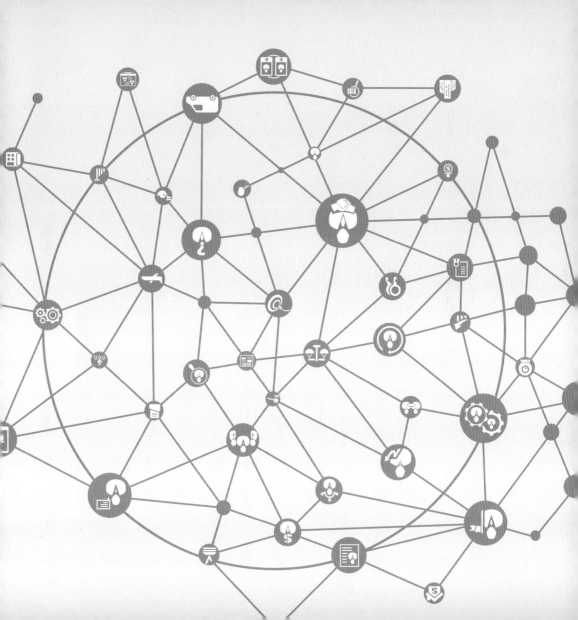

DEALING WITH TECHNOLOGY

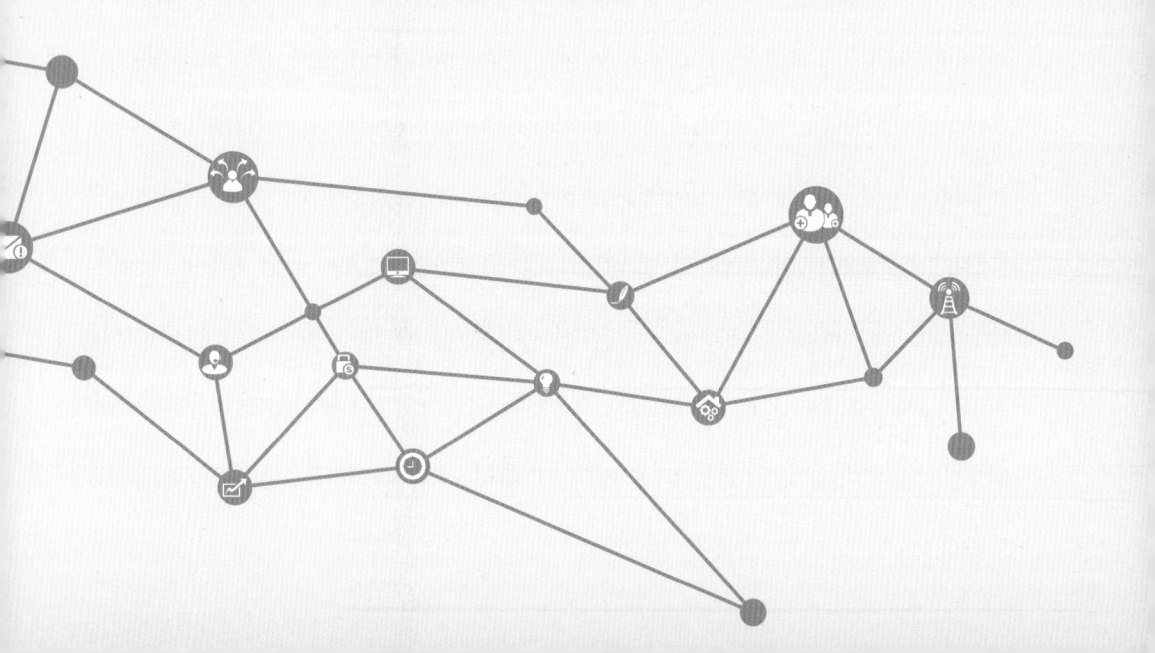

Yesterday we passed each other in the hall but you didn't look up because you were texting. This morning you came to the staff meeting with your smartphone. A quick glance told me you were checking tweets rather than taking notes. I understand technology has changed all our lives, but some of these applications are still hard for me to accept.

Humor me for a minute and let me reminisce about what it was like when I started out in the workplace. My parents gave me an electric typewriter when I started junior college. I marveled at its ability to create a **bold** font. (Only we didn't call it a font. It was simply "dark letters.") Résumés were always submitted on actual paper and often hand-delivered to where you were applying. If you really wanted a chance to stand out, you'd type on special résumé paper. When I started my first job, our team secretary (not administrative assistant) deciphered my

sloppy handwriting and typed everything I wrote. I left work at 5:00 p.m. and received work-related calls at home only if there was an extreme emergency. I even went on weeklong vacations without checking in at work even once!

Yes, that was back in the Stone Age, so you can see why it is sometimes hard for me to understand all the technology you use. It's hard for me to admit, but there are times that I just want to use paper and pencil to make a simple graph instead of creating an Excel spreadsheet. While you grew up with technology, I've had to take some classes and actually study to understand how technology helps us in all aspects of our lives. There's no denying technology can make us all more productive.

I realize technology is changing our personal and professional lives, so I want to stop complaining about this new way of getting things done. By listening to you (and learning from you) when it comes to

technology, we can create a more efficient and successful workplace. I enjoy seeing how quickly you learn to use and work with new gizmos, gadgets, and software. When presented with a problem, you immediately go online to watch a video, search a web page, or listen to a podcast to get the information you need. It's much more efficient than driving to the library and looking up something in an encyclopedia! You often serve as my role model by showing me the advantages of incorporating technology in our daily work.

I fully understand that staying on the cutting edge of technology helps us drive our organization forward. We keep up-to-date on the latest trends while hopefully surpassing our competitors. The world seems like a smaller place as we interconnect with each other using technology.

That said, all this technology still creates a steep learning curve for those of us who didn't begin using computers in preschool. Every day

I'm learning how efficient it is to collate data, research trends, and keep track of inventory using the tools technology gives us. We can conduct staff training online and create videos to attract customers. All these things happen at a faster pace than when I started my career. Technology, used correctly, is a way to be more efficient and productive. Who doesn't want that? We Boomers want advancement as much as you do.

Remember to be patient; we are trying to catch up and catch on at the same time!

Being ready isn't enough;
you have to be <u>prepared</u> for

a promotion or any other

significant change.

Pat Riley

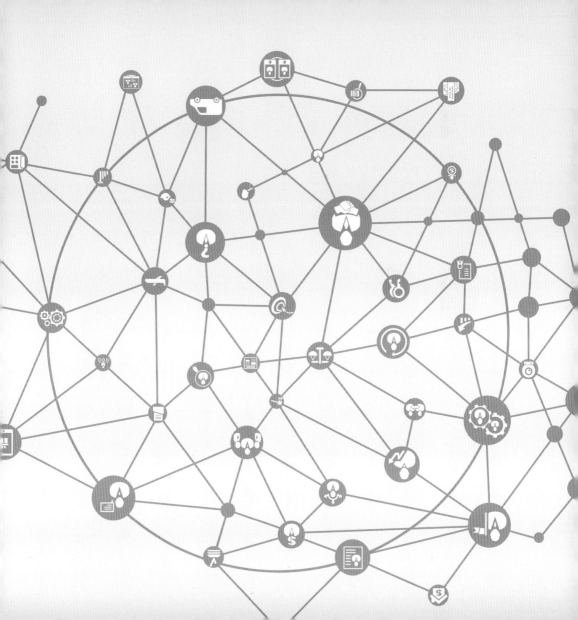

PROMOTION
AND
ADVANCEMENT

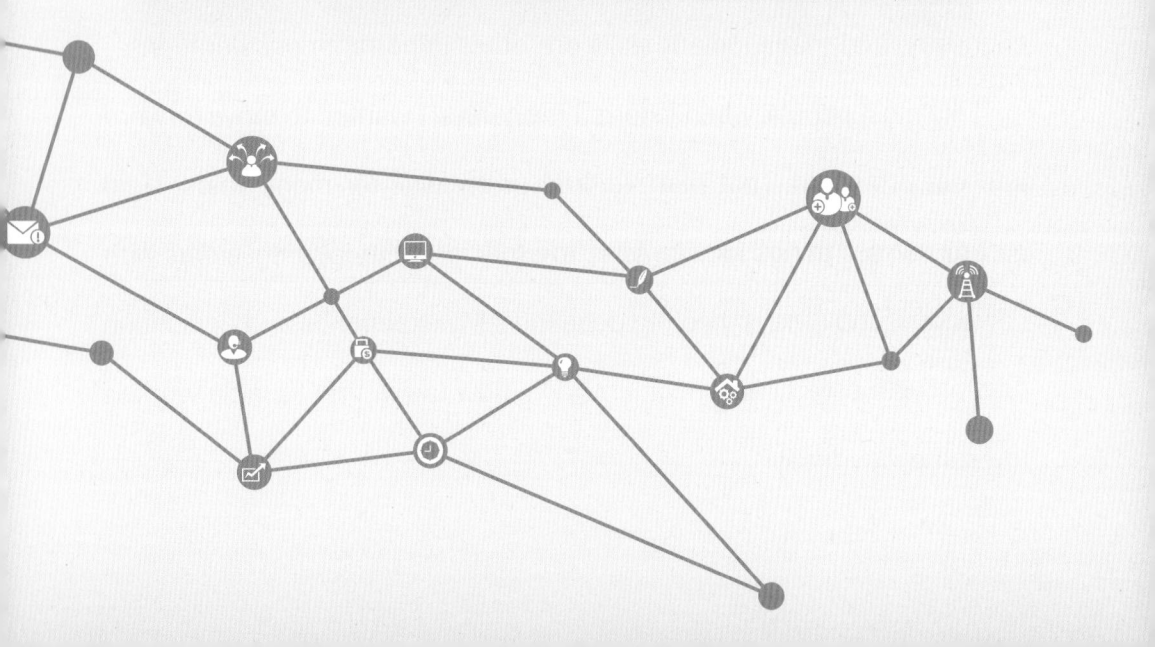

n some established and traditional organizations, promotions come on a regular basis. You do a good job and soon you are moving up the proverbial ladder. But what happens if you work for an organization where it seems as if promotions are randomly assigned and the most qualified people are not the ones selected for promotions? In the real world, job performance is just one of the criteria used for a person's selection to higher levels of responsibility. Factors such as creativity, chemistry, and management skills are other important considerations.

Like most people, when I started my career, I wanted to move forward and get promoted. That plan worked pretty well for many years. I did all the correct things like arriving to work on time, getting along with coworkers, and always meeting deadlines. My experience and dedication paid off with several advancements. Oh, how I wish that formula worked the same way today!

Today organizations see they can hire younger workers with much higher levels of walk-in technological knowledge. This puts me in an awkward position when I find that while my new supervisor has a master's degree, she has little actual professional experience. For me that means I need to adapt to this new world order, acquire the skills I need, or just sit back and complain that things are not like they use to be.

I fully recognize you and your colleagues have the skills and energy to make big things happen. However, I also believe your criteria for success are too narrow. To be successful and considered for advancement, you must have the technical talents of course, but you also need to have important skills in working collaboratively with people, building trust, and getting bottom-line results. In addition, you must also be able to clearly understand our current and future customer base, our competition, and have a keen understanding of internal and external best practices we can learn from and adopt.

This soapbox message aside, I know many of you want to develop and attain higher levels of responsibility. While the advancement "rules of the road" may be changing, many factors remain essential for your long-term success.

I have long learned that success is a blend of beliefs and behaviors from yesterday with the new and exciting ideas of today. We Boomers have a lot of life experiences that could be of help to you and your colleagues. Many of us would welcome the opportunity to share some of these thoughts and insights with you—you just have to ask!

Learn from those who have "been there and done that" sitting right next to you today. Most discussions of decision-making assume that only senior executives make decisions or that only senior executives' decisions matter. This is a dangerous mistake.

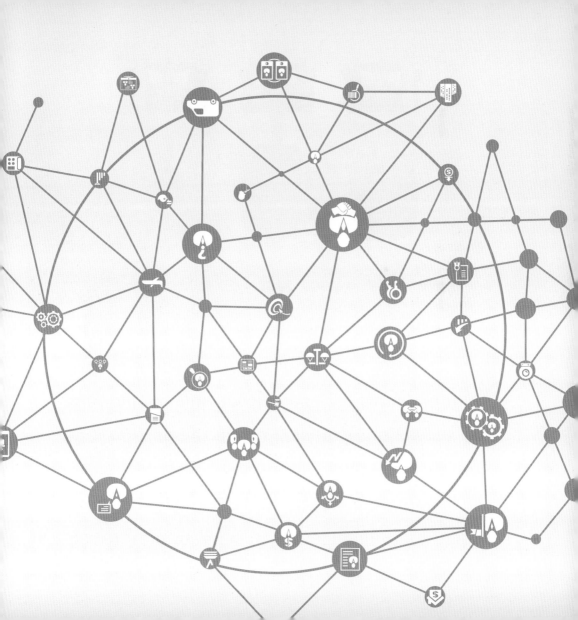

DECISION-MAKING

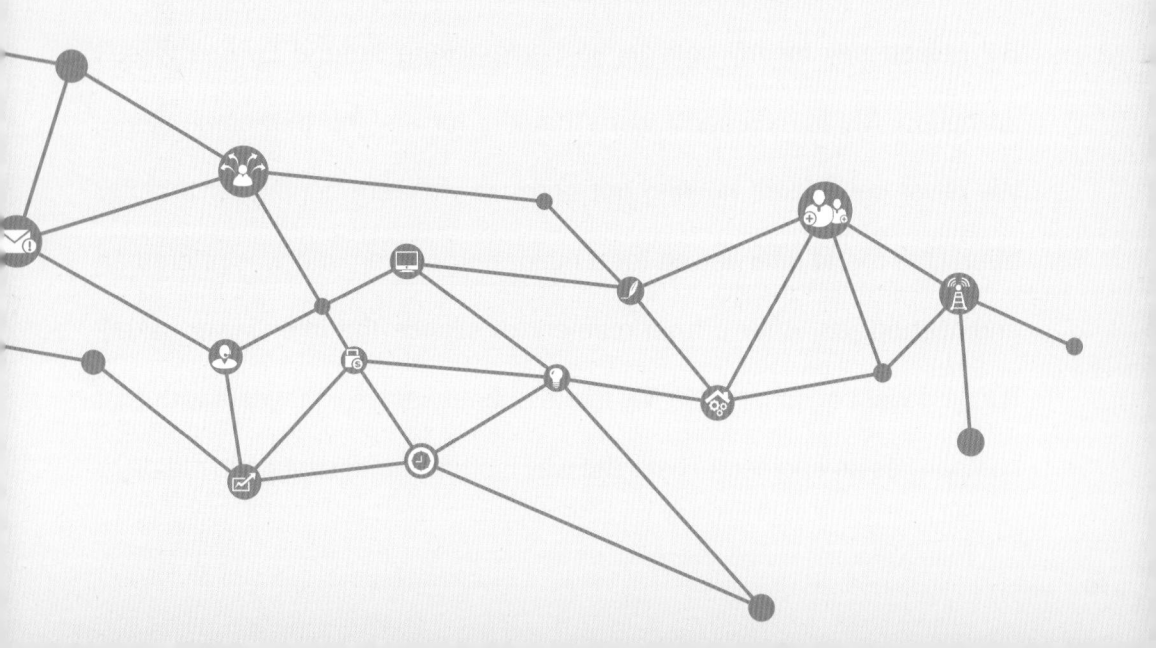

s it better to buy or lease a new car? Should I use my retirement funds to help pay for my daughter's college tuition? Is it financially wise to keep working at this organization even though my new boss is difficult? Should I retire early or work for a few more years? Decisions, decisions! We make decisions every day ranging from what type of coffee to order to selecting a nursing home for an aging parent.

Earlier in my career, choices were made out of necessity. The GI Bill helped pay for my college, so backpacking around Europe wasn't an option. My friends and I were thankful for any job that came along. We never considered holding out because we were hoping for a better offer. One friend interviewed for a major corporation and was offered an engineering job. After a brief moment of silence the interviewer asked, "Do you want a job or not?" My friend spent twenty-eight years with that company as an engineer! That's the way it often went in the good old days.

Research shows that decision-making processes change with age. Young adults typically focus on the negative results of their decisions. They think, "If I decide to take a gap year after high school, I might lose out on job offers" or "Buying a new car on credit means my credit score would plummet if I missed a payment." We all have different ways of analyzing how we make decisions. Many of us get so scared of making the wrong choice that we don't decide at all! Then another person or circumstance ends up making the choice for us.

Now that I'm older, I don't agonize as much over major and minor decisions. Sometimes it's enough to simply make a list of pros and cons and make a decision based on those points. No need to get paralyzed with fear that I might make the wrong choice. At this stage in my life, I look at the past decisions I've made and realize by using common sense that things have turned out pretty well.

When making a decision, I try to see the situation from different angles. Let's say I'm thinking about applying for a new position at work. If I apply for the promotion and get the job, will the extra work take me away from my family? If I apply and don't get the job, will I resent whoever gets the position? How will I feel next week if I don't even apply for the position? Going through different scenarios helps me make an educated decision.

As you make decisions in your life, try to find someone you respect to be your sounding board. They'll listen as you share the reasons why you want to quit your job or why you think you should confront a supervisor over a work-related incident. Sometimes just verbalizing your thoughts to another person helps you clear up the confusing thoughts swirling around in your head. Decision-making is hard! Sometimes a small decision makes a big impact on your life. Other times you might not make a decision and then later regret your decision not to do anything. By

establishing goals and setting our priorities, we can all make decisions that result in better outcomes.

Make decisions not just based on where you currently are, but rather on where you want to be.

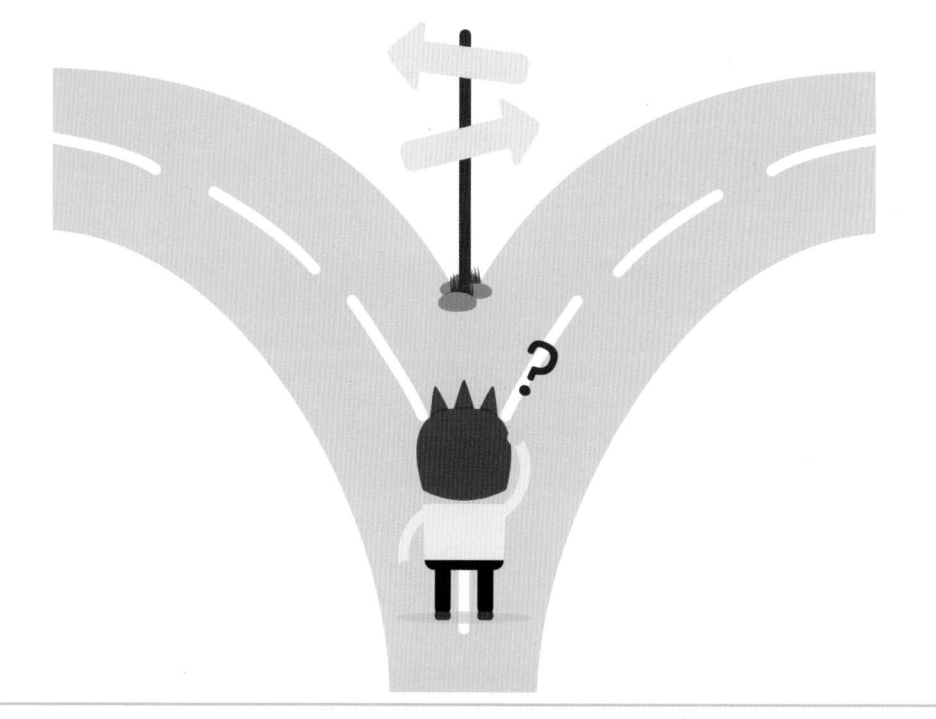

I follow three rules: do the right thing, do the best

you can, and always

show people you care.

Lou Holtz

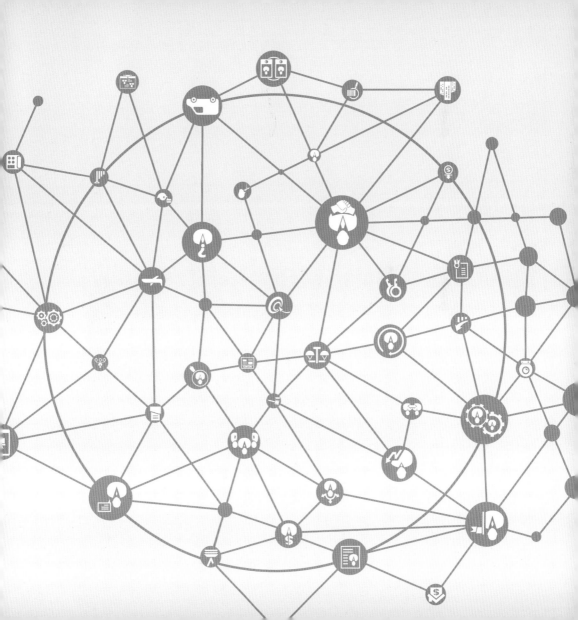

RULES
AND
REGULATIONS

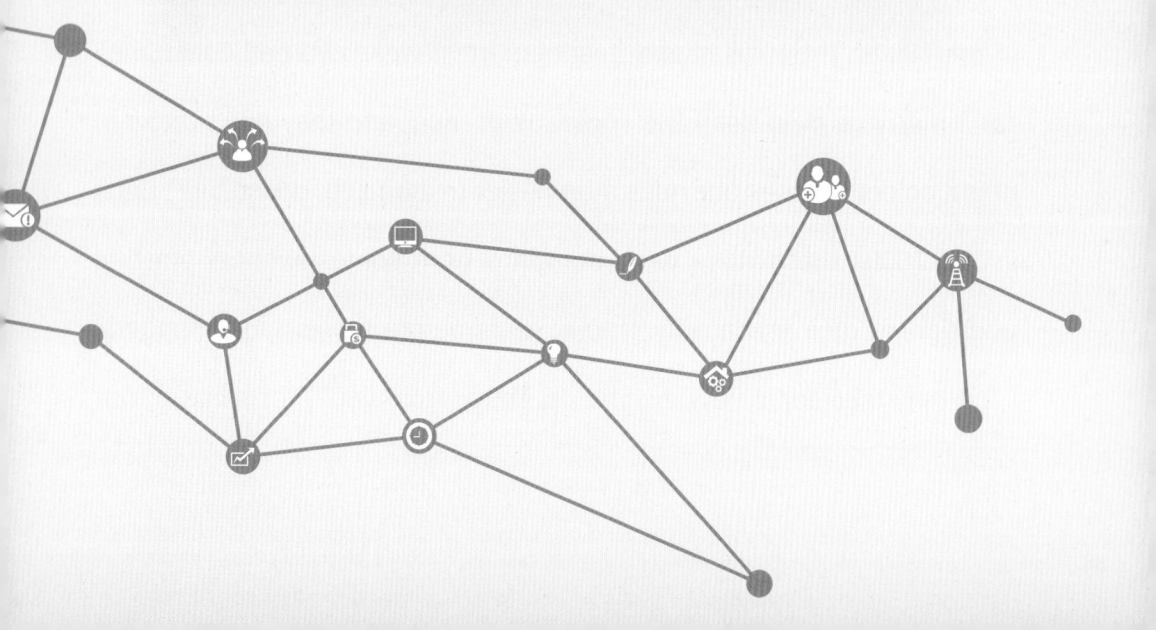

Sometimes, when my grandson resents me telling him to buckle his seat belt, he loudly proclaims, "You can't tell me what to do! You're not the boss of me!" In a sense, as his grandparent, I am his boss. I have years of maturity and life experiences that put me in a position to know a seat belt can save his life…even if it is uncomfortable.

In the workplace, some rules make employees uncomfortable. To Millennials some rules may even seem unnecessary and downright restrictive. Just imagine if you had to abide by the rules for a teacher in the 1800s. The rules stated: teachers must wear two petticoats, they can't marry or even keep the company of men, and they can't dress in bright colors! (Makes our rules a bit easier to stomach, doesn't it?) Back in the 1800s those rules were standard until some teachers starting questioning their practicality. It took years before those rules changed.

It may take some new insights (perhaps from you?) for some of our

rules to change, but in the meantime please abide by the rules we currently have.

Over the years, committees and teams spent hours deciding how and why we have certain policies and procedures; it doesn't make sense to disregard them on a whim. Perhaps we can discuss making changes after you've been with the organization for a while. Until that time, please don't arrive at work when you feel like it or decide to bring your dog because your friend's workplace allows pets. Yes, it would be comfortable to wear flip-flops and tank tops to work, but that attire may not appeal to our customers; without our customers, we are out of a job.

Every workplace has its own culture and "flavor." Some work in stodgy offices with a strict hierarchy of command. Others run offices where a casual atmosphere prevails with an open-door policy. Some organizations can create a very laid-back atmosphere. Yet each needs

some basic rules and regulations to be successful. Would it make sense to tell payroll you'll turn in your time sheet when you feel like it rather than on a designated day? If customers expect to buy their coffee at 7:00 a.m., we need rules requiring staff to be ready with freshly brewed coffee when the doors open. By having rules in place, employees as well as customers know what to expect. Employees expect to get paid on the first and third Friday of the month. Customers expect their phone call or email to get a response within twenty-four hours.

Wherever we work, rules and regulations help create a predictable environment. Could some rules be changed or even abolished? Of course! If there is a certain rule or regulation that you strongly believe needs changing, by all means, bring it up for consideration. You might point out ways to adapt or modify an existing rule so it works better for everyone. Perhaps we'll find some rules that have lost their relevancy. By working

together in this area we all gain new insight. After all, teachers today don't have to wear two petticoats!

Together let's learn why certain rules are needed, and see if changes could be made so we can all be more effective.

TEAMWORK

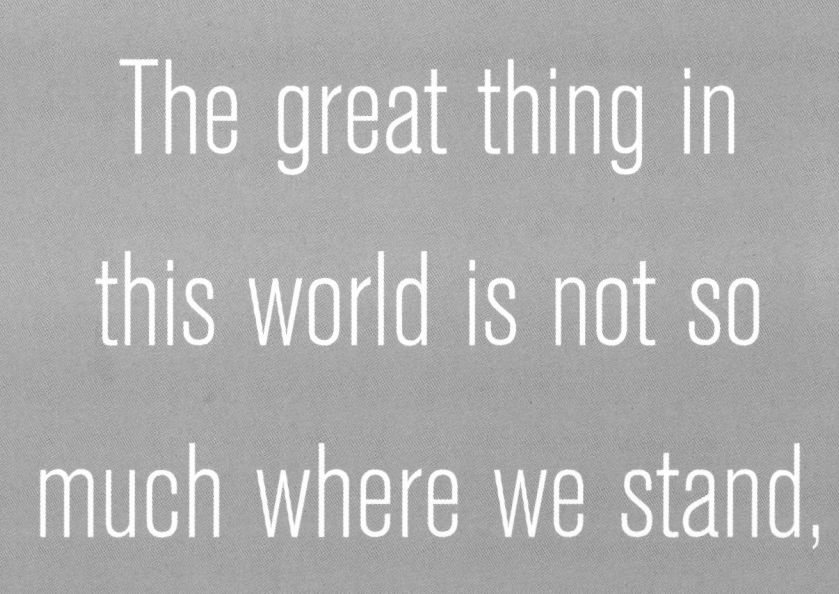

The great thing in
this world is not so
much where we stand,

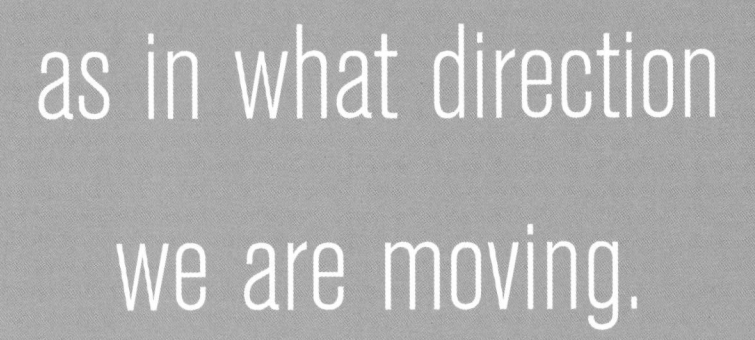

as in what direction
we are moving.

Oliver Wendell Holmes

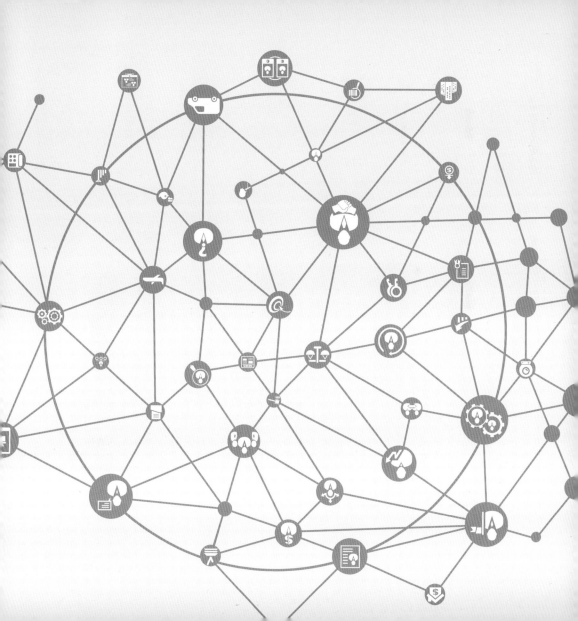

PERSONAL GROWTH AND DEVELOPMENT

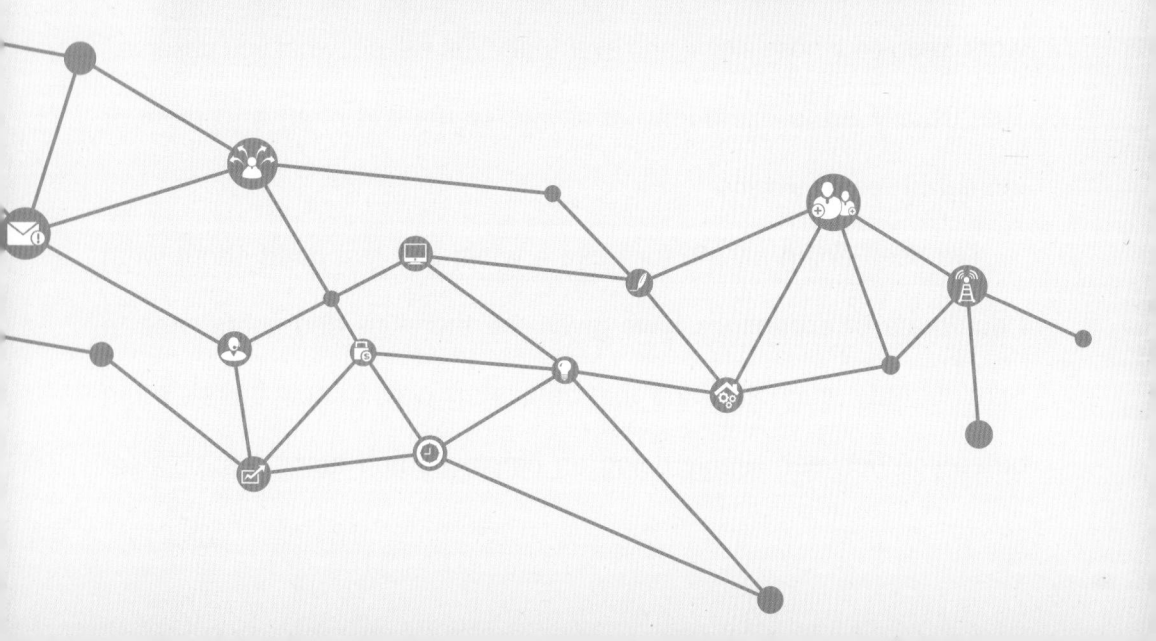

Back in the '80s, Robert Fulghum assured us that all we needed to know about life we learned in kindergarten. Eat cookies at snack time, be kind, and hold hands with your friends. What more did we have to do? There wasn't a need to continuously buy the self-help book of the week or walk over coals to find your inner self.

I understand the basic rules for development and advancement, and I remember a manager in the past telling me her philosophy: "Do good work, keep your nose clean, and eventually you will get what you deserve." That usually led to—although not always—some sort of advancement or increased responsibility.

I've been doing my job for quite a while and feel good about what I do. Years of experience have given me the skills and confidence to handle pretty much anything that comes my way. I know there's a big difference between simply being an employee and being a supervisor

who manages employees. I've learned through the school of hard knocks how to handle disgruntled coworkers and how to make myself valuable to the organization. Yet, I also understand the need to continue developing myself as an individual.

Along with attending the school of hard knocks, I've gone to conferences and read self-development books to keep me up-to-date on how to motivate myself and others. I've even taken a few personality tests to see where I need improvement when it comes to communicating with my staff and colleagues. (One test revealed I definitely need to give less advice and do more listening.) Personal growth and development is a continuous and challenging process that reaps big rewards.

I've also learned a few things about personal development and the first rule is **don't wait**. Don't wait for others to take you under their wings and feed you what you will need to learn, advance, and, if you

desire, get promoted to increasing levels of responsibility. Here are a few growth and personal development rules of the road:

- Be fully familiar with our organization's mission and goals.

- Constantly look for ways to do your job more effectively and help others do the same.

- Take specific actions to ensure you continue to learn, grow, and apply new skills.

- Ask me and my Boomer buddies to assist you on your personal and professional development goals. Take advantage of the fact that we have some valuable life lessons that could be of help to you. We would happily share these experiences with you, so please ask!

Here's the deal. Both Boomers and Millennials miss opportunities for personal growth and development, and that can't continue if we really care about our future. Both of our groups need to be much more proactive to achieve our shared goals.

Let's look for developmental opportunities so we can succeed together.

Coming together

is a beginning;

keeping together

is progress;

WORKING TOGETHER
IS SUCCESS.

Henry Ford

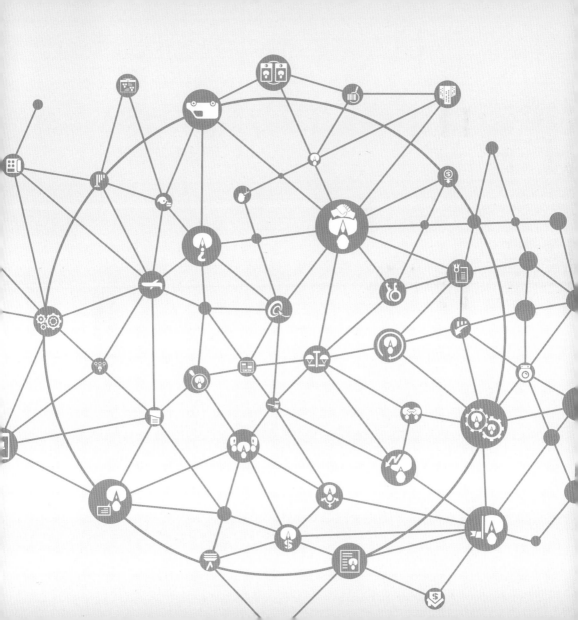

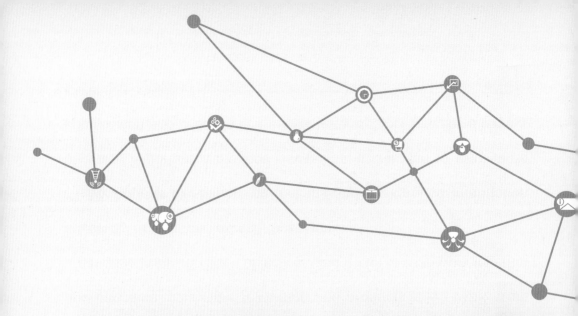

WHAT ARE
THESE MESSAGES
REALLY ABOUT?

Before you assume this book and my shared viewpoints are nothing more than a list of gripes and "woe is me" complaints, let me be clear. They are, in fact, just the opposite. My goal here is to not only set the record straight but to use this shared information to build more understanding, support, and acceptance with you and your Millennial colleagues.

Having diverse viewpoints can make the workplace more enjoyable and enriching, plus more rewarding and productive. We work in an organization with important objectives, and it's up to us to work together effectively to meet and exceed those goals.

My hope is by sharing my feelings and background information on these important workplace viewpoints, it will lead to even more appreciation and collaboration between my Boomer buddies and your Millennial cohorts.

On the future

My excitement about the future stems mostly from the hope that it will produce many more opportunities for both of us to advance, grow, and achieve the personal fulfillment we all seek. My anxiety comes from the simple fear of the unknown. It comes from a deep concern that I may not be able to respond to all the changes that are happening in business today. Some of them will be easy for me to embrace and implement. Others will require great change and new learning on my part—and patience on the part of others to include you.

Do I have all the answers? **No.** In fact, I often have more questions than answers. However, I do know this: Yesterday is gone. The future is what we both have to work with, and the future begins today!

Anxious about the future? Just know you are not alone.

What I ask of you:

- Appreciate the fact that my challenges are no easier than yours and my viewpoints are not wrong—just different.

- Don't assume I am "stuck in my ways" and unable or un- willing make changes.

- Continue to challenge attitudes and behaviors, including mine, that can be enhanced and improved.

- Adopt the mind-set that for you to be successful at work you need me as much as I need you.

- Assume half the responsibility for our working relationship. If we make improvements together, take half the credit. If

we don't make improvements, accept half the responsibility for making it better.

And when you do, I believe you will find…
With more understanding
And greater appreciation
We can meet in the middle
And succeed together.

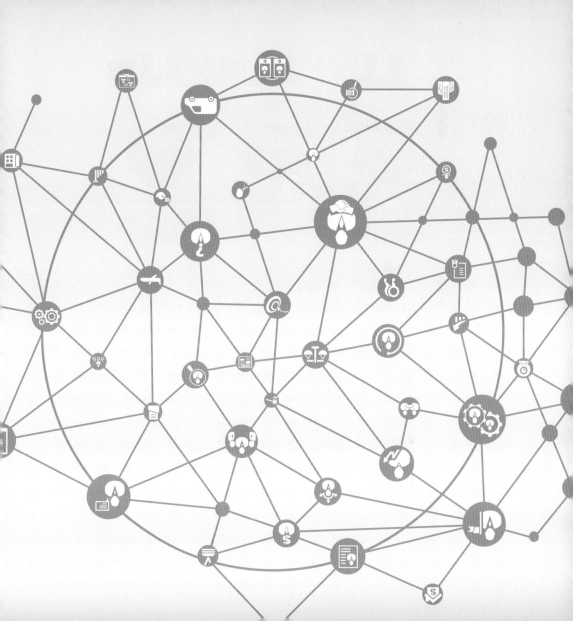

ABOUT THE AUTHORS

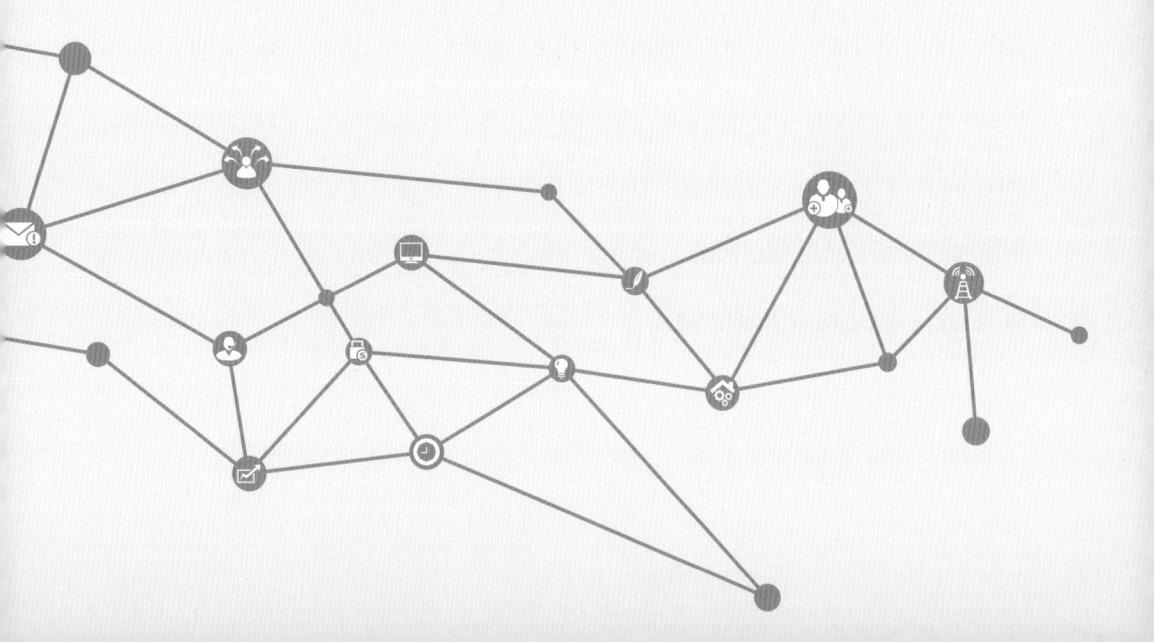

Eric Harvey is founder and president of the Walk the Talk Company and a leading expert on high-achieving leaders and organizations. Since its founding in 1977, Walk the Talk has worked with thousands of organizations worldwide, including multinational corporations, leading health care providers, high-tech start-ups, and highly respected nonprofit organizations. Eric has authored twenty-five books that have sold millions of copies, including the bestsellers *Walk the Talk, Ethics 4 Everyone, Walk Awhile in My Shoes*, and *Go for the Gold*. He and his wife, Nancy, live in Pensacola Beach, Florida, and are the proud parents of two daughters and have six grandchildren.

Silvana Clark spent six weeks living with 120 Millennials to start her research for this book. Before that, she wrote twelve books, carried the torch for the 2012 Olympics (not for her athletic prowess!), appeared on Fox's *Trading Spouses*, and spent nineteen months living and working from a branded RV. A professional speaker, Silvana travels the country giving motivational keynotes and presentations on how businesses can benefit from harnessing the energy and skills of Millennials.

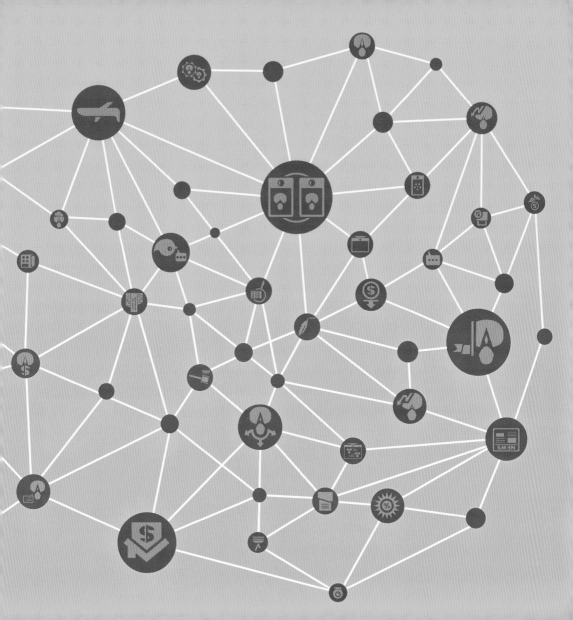